THE
CONSTITUTION
AND
LAWS
OF THE
CHOCTAW NATION.

SR Scholarly Resources Inc.
1508 Pennsylvania Avenue · Wilmington, Delaware 19806

SCHOLARLY RESOURCES, INC.
Wilmington, Delaware • London

Reprint edition published in 1975

Library of Congress Catalog Card Number: 75-3681
ISBN: 0-8420-1847-6

Manufactured in the United States of America

THE

CONSTITUTION

AND

LAWS

OF THE

CHOCTAW NATION.

PARK HILL, CHEROKEE NATION:
MISSION PRESS: EDWIN ARCHER, PRINTER.
1847.

CONSTITUTION OF THE CHOCTAW NATION.

We, the People of the Choctaw Nation, having a right to establish our own form of Government, not inconsistent with the Constitution, Treaties and Laws of the United States: by our Representatives assembled in Convention at Nanih-waiya on Thursday the tenth day of November, 1842, in order to establish Justice, insure Tranquillity, promote the general Welfare and secure to ourselves and our Posterity the right of Life, Liberty and Property: We mutually agree with each other to form for ourselves a free and independent Government.

And we do hereby recognize the boundaries assigned the Choctaw Nation by the second article of the Treaty made and concluded with United States of America, at Dancing Rabbit Creek, on the 27th of September, 1830: viz. beginning near Fort Smith, where the Arkansas boundary crosses the Arkansas River, running thence to the source of the Canadian Fork, if in the limits of the United States, or to those limits; thence due South to Red River, thence down Red River to the western boundary of the State of Arkansas, thence North along that line to the beginning; the boundary of the same to be agreeable to the Treaty made and concluded at Washington City in the year 1825.

DISTRICT BOUNDARIES.

For the convenience and good government of the people of the Choctaw Nation, We make and ordain and establish four Districts in this Nation, to be known by the following names and boundaries: viz. Mushulitubbi District, Apakshanubbi District, Pushimataha District and Chickasaw District.

The boundary line of Mushulitubbi District shall begin near Fort Smith where the Arkansas boundary crosses the Arkansas River, thence up said River to the Canadian Fork to where the Chickasaw District boundary strikes the same, thence along the said Chickasaw District boundary to where it strikes the dividing ridge between the Canadian and Red River, thence Eastwardly along said dividing ridge to the Western boundary of the State of Arkansas, thence along said Arkansas line to the beginning.

The boundary of Apakshanubbi District shall begin on Red River where the Arkansas State line strikes the same, running thence up said River to the mouth of Kiamichi, thence up said River to Jack's Fork, thence up said Jack's Fork to the Military Road leading from Fort Smith to Horse Prairie, thence along said Military Road to the boundary line of Mushulitubbi District on the top of the dividing ridge between the Arkansas and Red Rivers, thence Eastwardly along said District boundary to the Western boundary of the State of Arkansas, thence along said boundary of the State of Arkansas to the beginning.

The boundary of Pushimataha District shall begin on Red River at the mouth of Kiamichi, thence running up said Red River to the mouth of Island Bayou to where the Chickasaw District boundary strikes said River, thence along said Chickasaw District boundary to the dividing ridge between the Red and Canadian Rivers, thence Eastwardly along the line of Mushulitubbi District on the top of the dividing ridge to where the district line of Apakshanubbi District intersects Mushulitubbi District, thence South along said Apakshanubbi District line to the beginning.

The Chickasaw District shall be bounded as follows: viz. beginning on the North bank of Red River at the mouth of Island Bayou about eight or ten miles below the mouth of False Washita, thence running North along the main channel of said Bayou to its source, thence along the dividing ridge to the road leading from Fort Gibson to Fort Washita, thence along said road to the line dividing Mushulitubbi and Pushimataha Districts, thence Eastwardly along said district line to the source of Brushy Creek, thence down said Creek to where it flows into the Canadian, thence West along said Canadian River to its source, if in the limits of the United

States, and thence due South to Red River and down Red River to the beginning.

ARTICLE 1.

DECLARATION OF RIGHTS.

SEC. 1. All freemen when they form a Social Compact are equal in rights; and no man, or set of men, are entitled to exclusive separate public emoluments or privileges but in consideration of public services.

SEC. 2. All political power is inherent in the people, and free governments are founded on their authority and instituted for their benefit; and therefore they have at all times an inalienable and indefeasible right to alter, reform or abolish their form of government in such manner as they think expedient.

SEC. 3. There shall be no establishment of religion by law. No preference shall ever be given by law to any religious sect, society, denomination or mode of worship, and no religious test shall ever be allowed as a qualification to any public trust under this government.

SEC. 4. No human authority ought in any case whatever to control or interfere with the rights of conscience.

SEC. 5. No person shall for the same offence be twice put in jeopardy of life or limbs, nor shall any person's property be taken or applied to any public use, unless just compensation be made therefor.

SEC. 6. No title of nobility or hereditary distinction, privileges, honour or emolument shall ever be granted or conferred under this government, nor shall an office be created, the appointment of which shall be for a longer time than during good behavior.

SEC. 7. The right of trial by jury shall remain inviolate.

SEC. 8. Every citizen has a right to bear arms in defence of himself and his country.

ARTICLE 2.

DISTRIBUTION OF POWERS.

SEC. 1. The powers of the Government of the Choctaw

Nation shall be divided into three distinct departments, and each of them confined to a separate body of magistracy: viz. those which are legislative to one, those which are executive to another, and those which are judicial to another.

Sec. 2. No person or collection of persons, being one of those departments, shall exercise any power properly belong ing to either of the others, except in the instances hereinafter expressly directed or permitted by the General Council.

ARTICLE 3.

LEGISLATIVE DEPARTMENT.

Sec. 1. The legislative power of this Nation shall be vested in a General Council, which shall consist of a Senate and House of Representatives, and the style of their laws shall be: *Be it enacted by the General Council of the Choctaw Nation assembled.*

Sec. 2. The Senate of the Choctaw Nation shall be composed of three Senators from each District, chosen by the qualified electors for the term of two years.

Sec. 3. No person shall be a Senator who shall not have attained to the age of thirty years, and been one year a citizen of this Nation, and who shall not when elected be an inhabitant of that District for which he shall be chosen.

Sec. 4. No person shall be a Senator unless he be a natural born citizen of this Nation.

Sec. 5. The Senate shall choose a President from its own body, who shall have no vote unless they be equally divided.

Sec. 6. The Senate shall choose its other officers.

Sec. 7. The General Council shall have the sole power to try all impeachments; when sitting for that purpose they shall be on oath or affirmation, and no person shall be convicted without two-thirds of both branches of the General Council.

Sec. 8. Judgment in cases of impeachment shall not extend further than removal from office; but the parties charged with any crime shall nevertheless, before or after impeachment, be liable to indictment, trial, judgment and punishment according to law; and when charges for impeachment are preferred, the person or persons so charged shall be duly notified by the light-horse-men, by the order of the Chief, to attend the General Council, that his trial may be fair and impartial.

Sec. 9. The times and places of holding elections for Chiefs, Senators, Representatives and other officers shall be prescribed by law.

Sec. 10. The House of Representatives shall be composed of members chosen every year by the qualified electors in the several Districts at the ratio of one Representative to every one thousand citizens; nevertheless, when there is a fractional number exceeding five hundred citizens in any District, they shall be entitled to one additional Representative. No person shall be a Representative unless he be a citizen of the Choctaw Nation, or who shall have not have attained to the age of twenty-one years, or who shall not when elected be an inhabitant of that District in which he shall be chosen.

Sec. 11. In case of the death, resignation or inability of any of the Senators or Representatives from the several Districts, the District Chief or his Speaker shall have power to make temporary appointments until the next election.

Sec. 12. The Senators and Representatives shall receive for their services such compensation as may be determined by the General Council, and paid out of the national funds.

Sec. 13. Each House shall be the judge of the election returns and qualifications of its own members, and a majority of each House shall constitute a quorum to do business.

Sec. 14. Bills may originate in either House, and be amended, altered or rejected by the other; but no bill shall have the force of a law until it shall have passed by a majority of both branches of the General Council; and every one having passed by both branches of the General Council shall be signed by the Speaker and President of their respective bodies.

Sec. 15. Every bill which shall have passed the General Council shall be presented to the Chiefs or Speakers; if they approve it, they shall sign it, and it shall become a law; if not, they shall return it to the branch in which it originated, with their objections. The General Council shall then reconsider it, and if repassed by two-thirds of both branches it shall become a law as if the Chiefs had signed it.

SEC. 16. The House of Representatives when assembled shall choose a Speaker and its other officers, and when a majority of the members are assembled it shall constitute a quorum to do business.

SEC. 17. The General Council may determine the rules of its own proceedings, and punish a member or other persons for disorderly conduct or behavior; and shall keep a journal of its proceedings, and cause a true copy of the same to be sent to each District.

SEC. 18. The General Council of the Choctaw Nation shall assemble at least once in every year, and such meeting shall be at Nanihwaiya on the first Wednesday in October every year.

SEC. 19. The Yeas and Nays of the members of the General Council on any question shall, at the request of any three members present, be entered on the journal.

ARTICLE 4.

EXECUTIVE DEPARTMENT.

SEC. 1. The Supreme power of this Nation shall be vested in four District Chiefs; any two of them shall be deemed sufficient to exercise the duties of the Executive at the General Council.

SEC. 2. The Chiefs of the several Districts shall hold their office for the term of four years from the time of their installation until their successors shall be duly elected; but shall not be eligible for the same office for more than two terms in succession.

SEC. 3. The District Chiefs and their Speakers shall be elected by the qualified electors in their respective Districts; but in case of death, resignation, removal or inability of any of the Chiefs, the Speaker shall exercise the duties of the

Chief until [a new Chief shall be chosen at] the next July election, which Chief when elected shall only serve out the time of the remaining term. The General Council shall have the power by law to determinethe compensation of the Chiefs and Speakers of the several Districts.

SEC. 4. No person except a natural born citizen of the Choctaw Nation shall be eligible to the office of Chief, neither shall any person be eligible to that office, who shall not have attained to the age of thirty years, and been an inhabitant of the District from which he shall be chosen at least one year.

SEC. 5. Each Chief from time to time shall give the General Council information respecting the affairs of his own District, and recommend to their consideration such measures as he may deem expedient, and they shall take care that the laws be faithfully executed in their respective Districts.

SEC. 6. The District Chiefs before they enter upon the duties of their respective offices shall take the following oath or affirmation: viz, "I do solemnly swear or affirm that I will to the best of my judgment and ability faithfully execute the duties of my office, and will preserve, protect and defend the Constitution of the Choctaw Nation."

SEC. 7. Each Chief shall have the right to appoint his own District Secretary and the Light-horse-men within his District.

SEC. 8. Any two of the District Chiefs shall have power on extraordinary occasions to convene the General Council at Nanihwaiya, but such called Sessions shall not take place more than once in any one year.

SEC. 9. There shall be an election held for District Chief and Speaker in Apakshanubbi District on the second Wednesday in July, 1844, which Chief and Speaker when elected shall serve only two years; there shall be also an election held in Pushimataha District for Chief and Speaker on the second Wednesday in July, 1845, which Chief and Speaker when elected shall serve only one year; and on the second Wednesday in July, 1846, there shall be an election held for the District Chief and Speaker in the several Distiicts of the Choctaw Nation, and at the end of every subsequent period of four years there shall be an election held for District Chief and Speaker throughout the Choctaw Nation.

SEC. 10. During the absence of any of the District Chiefs his Speaker shall exercise the duties of Chief.

ARTICLE 5.

JUDICIAL DEPARTMENT.

SEC. 1. The judicial power of this Nation shall be vested in a National, and Supreme and Inferior District Courts.

SEC. 2. The National Court shall be composed of one National Judge together with the Supreme Judges of the several Districts, who shall sit and hold the National Court at Nanihwaiya during the Session of the General Council.

SEC. 3. The National Judge together with any two or more of the Supreme Judges, or any three of the Supreme Judges, shall be sufficient to constitute the National Court of the Choctaw Nation, and whose decision shall be ultimate and final.

SEC. 4. The National Judge and Supreme District Judges shall be elected by the General Council, and hold their offices during good behaviour.

SEC. 5. No person except a natural born citizen shall be eligible to the office of National Judge, and who shall not have attained to the age of thirty years.

SEC. 6. The Supreme District Court shall be composed of one Superior District Judge, with from one to four inferior Associate Judges composed of the Judges of the Inferior Courts, and the Inferior Courts shall be composed of one Judge to each Court.

SEC. 7. The Inferior District Judges shall receive their appointments from the District Chiefs in their respective Districts, and hold their office during good behaviour.

SEC. 8. No person who shall not have attained to the age of twenty-five years, shall be eligible to the office of Supreme District Judge.

SEC. 9. The General Council shall have the power by law to designate the times and places of holding Supreme and

Inferior Courts, also to prescribe the manner in which the Courts of this Nation shall be conducted.

SEC. 10. All trials in the District Courts shall be by jury composed of twelve free disinterested citizens of the Choctaw Nation, who shall all agree in a verdict.

SEC. 11. In all trials by jury the Judge shall empannel at Court twenty-four disinterested men, out of which the defendant shall have the right to select twelve jurors to decide the case in suit.

SEC. 12. No Judge shall sit on the trial of any Court when the parties or either of them shall be connected with him by affinity or consanguinity, or when he may be interested in the same, except by consent of the parties, and whenever a case in Court is so situated as aforesaid, one of the Judges of the Inferior Court shall preside for the determination thereof.

SEC. 13. In all trials of capital and criminal cases, the defendant alone shall have the right of an appeal from an Inferior Court to a Supreme Court within the District, or the Supreme Court of another District, and from thence to the National Court; but in all civil cases either party shall have the right of an appeal in the manner aforesaid: *Provided*, the Judge of such Court or Courts shall be satisfied that ample justice has not been done to the party seeking an appeal, and they shall grant it.

SEC. 14. The Judges of the Courts of this Nation shall receive for their services such compensation to be fixed by law which shall not be diminished during their continuance in office.

SEC. 15. There shall be District Attornies elected in each District by the qualified electors of their respective Districts, whose compensation and term of service shall be prescribed by law.

ARTICLE 6.

GENERAL PROVISIONS.

SEC. 1. The Choctaw Nation shall not after the adoption

of this Constitution be responsible to pay any debt or debts of individuals, and no money shall ever be taken from the General Annuity of the Nation to be applied to any purpose whatever unless by special appropriation of the General Council.

SEC. 2. The citizens of any of the Districts of the Choctaw Nation shall be entitled to all the privileges and immunities of citizenship in the several Districts.

SEC. 3. All just debts that may have been contracted by citizens of this Nation previous to the adoption of this Constitution shall remain in full force and virtue against them.

SEC. 4. A person charged in any District with felony or other crime, who shall flee from justice, and be found in another District, shall, on demand by the Chief of the District from which he fled, be delivered up by the Chief of the District in which he may be found, to be removed for trial to the District having jurisdiction of the crime.

SEC. 5. The General Council shall have the power to pass such laws and measures as they shall deem expedient for the general good of the Nation: *Provided*, No law be passed or adopted contrary to the provisions of this Constitution.

SEC. 6. From and after the adoption of this Constitution, no free negro, or any part negro, unconnected with Choctaw and Chickasaw blood, shall be permitted to come and settle in the Choctaw Nation.

SEC. 7. When offenders against the laws of this Nation are arraigned for trial, they shall be at liberty to defend their own case, or employ counsel, or both, that their trial may be fair and impartial.

SEC. 8. The mode of declaring war in this Nation, shall be by at least two-thirds of the members of the General Council, in full Council, with the approval of at least two of the District Chiefs or their Speakers, unless in the case of actual invasion by an enemy; in which case the people shall have the right to defend themselves until the Council is convened.

SEC. 9. When a person shall be elected a member to the

General Council, his term of service shall not expire until the next election day.

Sec. 10. The District Chiefs shall have the power, by the advice and consent of the General Council, to appoint Commissioners or Delegates to transact such business as may become expedient to the Choctaw Nation, and all other officers whose appointments are not herein otherwise provided for.

Sec. 11. The General Council of the Choctaw Nation shall have the power to pass such laws as they may think expedient, to punish rebellion, treason and other high crimes against the Nation.

Sec. 12. No person who is any part negro shall ever be allowed to hold any office under this Government.

Sec. 13. The General Council shall have the power by law to naturalize and adopt as citizens of this Nation any Indian or descendant of an Indian, except a negro or descendant of a negro, but who on petition to the General Council, giving satisfactory proof of good character, the Council may permit them to live in the Nation.

Sec. 14. There shall be a Treasurer and Auditor elected by the General Council for each District, whose duty shall be prescribed by law, and who shall hold their office two years, until their successors shall be duly elected and qualified.

Sec. 15. All contested elections shall be determined by the General Council.

Sec. 16. Members to the General Council, and all officers, both executive and judicial, shall be bound by an oath or affirmation to support the Constitution of this Nation, and to perform the duties of their respective offices with faithfulness and fidelity.

Sec. 17. The General Council shall have the power to prescribe by law the mode of keeping and disbursing the District funds.

Sec. 18. At the next July election there shall be thirty Captains elected by the qualified electors in Apakshanubbi

District, fifteen each in Mushulitubbi, Pushimataha and Chickasaw Districts, whose term of office shall be four years, subject to re-election, and whose duty shall be to see that justice is done to every individual at the payment of annuities, and use exertions, both by example and precept, to induce the people to live soberly, industriously and peaceably among one another in observance of the laws of their country. The compensation of Captains shall be determined by law.

Sec. 19. Eighteen thousand dollars of the interest money arising from the Chickasaw funds, granted to the Choctaws by convention held and concluded at Doaksville, shall, after the year of 1842, be set apart annually for educational purposes, and the remaining seven thousand dollars shall be set apart annually to be expended for blacksmith shops and other national purposes.

Sec. 20. The General Council shall have power to create by law such Regulations, Commissioners, Superintendents or such other officers as the case may require for the promotion and advancement of all the schools in the Nation.

MILITIA.

Sec. 21. The Gėneral Council shall have power by law for organizing and disciplining the Militia of this Nation in such manner as they shall deem expedient, not incompatible with the Constitution, Treaties and Laws of the United States in relation thereto.

Sec. 22. The Chief shall have power to call forth the Militia to execute the laws of the Nation, to suppres insurrection and repel invasion.

Sec. 23. All suits at law or in equity now pending in the several courts in this Nation may be transferred to such courts as may have proper jurisdiction thereof.

Sec. 24. No citizen of this Nation shall ever be required to pay poll, tax or be required to taxation for any property or for any pursuit of business whatever.

Sec. 25. Any citizen of this Nation who may find any mine or mines or mineral water, shall have exclusive right and privilege so long as he may choose to work the same, within one mile in any direction from his work or improvement: *Provided*, *however*, He does not interfere with the rights of a former settler.

Sec. 26. In all elections by the people it shall be in the following manner: viz. the name of each candidate shall be written in a separate column by the district secretary, naming the office or offices for which the candidates are running, and the name of every voter carefully written out in full and polled, inserting his vote in the same column in which the names of the candidates for whom he voted are placed, and the district secretary with two more temporary clerks appointed by the Supreme Judge, or any one of the Inferior Judges shall be authorized to act at every election, and those three shall each write down the name of every voter as directed above. When the polling is completed they shall carefully compare their copies together and count the votes, and if they prove correct the District Secretary shall proclaim on the ground how the votes stand, and who are elected.

Sec. 27. When there are several candidates running together for the same office, and out of them only a choice is to be made, the one having the highest number of votes shall be elected; but when several selections are to be made, as in the case of the members to the General Council, those only of the required number of votes shall be elected; but in case of a tie a new election shall immediately be made of the persons in tie.

Sec. 28. The Supreme District Judge with any one or two Judges of the Inferior Court, or they alone, shall preside over the elections as judges to see that the election be done fairly and correctly.

Sec. 29. Every male citizen of the Choctaw Nation at the age of sixteen years and upwards, who shall be an inhabitant of the Choctaw Nation, and shall have resided in the District at least one month, shall be deemed a qualified elector.

Sec. 30. The District Chiefs shall have power to remove any person for misdemeanor in office under their appointment.

SEC. 31. There shall be no retrospective law or any law passed under this Constitution impairing the obligation of contracts.

SEC. 32. In case of death, resignation or inability of any of the Supreme District Judges and District Attornies, the Chief shall have the power to make temporary appointments until the time arrives for appointing or electing such officers.

SEC. 33. The National Judge or any one of the Supreme District Judges shall administer the oath of office to any of the several officers in this Nation. The Chief shall be required to take the oath of office at Nanihwaiya in the presence of the General Council.

SEC. 34. The jurors shall take the following oath: "We do solemnly swear in the presence of God, that we will to the best of our judgment render a verdict according to law, justice, and the evidence which may be tending the case now before us."

We do declare and ordain that all the provisions contained in the Constitution of 1838, not revised and adopted by the Convention of 1842, are hereby null and void, and that there shall be no alterations made in this Constitution until the annual meeting of the General Council in the year of 1850; and that any law which may be passed contrary to the provisions of this Constitution shall be null and void, and all right and power not herein granted or expressed shall be reserved unto the people

LAWS.

[Repealed laws are omitted; and amended laws are printed as amended.]

SESSION I.—1834.

AN ACT preventing the introduction of whiskey.

SEC. 1. *Be it enacted by the General Council of the Choctaw Nation assembled*, That no person or persons shall be permitted to bring any whiskey or other ardent spirits into this Nation; and any person so offending shall have the whiskey or other ardent spirits destroyed by the light-horse-men or any one of them; and the captains and their warriors of the several districts shall have the power, and be bound to exercise the duties of the light-horse-men in assisting to destroy any whiskey or other ardent spirits which may be brought into the Nation.

And be it further enacted, That should any person or persons refuse to have his or her whiskey or other ardent spirits destroyed by taking up arms, and should any one of the light-horse-men, captains or warriors, in self-defence, kill or destroy the life of the person or persons having whiskey or other ardent spirits, he shall be protected by the laws of this Nation. But should any offender kill or destroy the life of any person or persons who are engaged in assisting to destroy the whiskey or other ardent spirits, such shall suffer death; but should the offender only destroy or injure the property or limbs of any of the light-horse-men, captains or warriors, he or she shall be liable to a fine or punishment according to the crime.

Approved October, 1834.

By JOSEPH KINCAID,
THOMAS LEFLORE,
NITAKACHE,
Chiefs.

AN ACT for punishing theft.

SEC. 2. *Be it enacted, &c.*, That any person or persons who shall take or steal any property, goods or chattels, shall return said property, goods or chattels so stolen or pay the value thereof, and shall receive such corporeal punishment as may be adequate to the theft, to be determined by twelve jurors: *Provided*, That no one shall receive at any time more than thirty-nine lashes on the bare back.

Approved October, 1834.

AN ACT making the killing a person for a witch a capital offence.

SEC. 3. *Be it enacted, &c.*, That any person or persons who shall kill another for a witch or wizard shall suffer death. And any person who shall publicly state that he himself or she herself is a witch or wizard, or shall say that such a person or persons are witches or wizards, and he or she knows it to be so, shall receive sixty lashes on the bare back.

Approved November 6, 1834.

AN ACT respecting Wills.

SEC. 4. *Be it enacted, &c.*, That all Wills made either verbally or in writing in the presence of two or more witnesses shall be valid to all intents and purposes.

Approved November, 1834.

AN ACT providing for the punishment of wilful murder.

SEC. 5. *Be it enacted, &c.*, That any person or persons who shall commit wilful murder shall suffer death; and the mode of of execution shall be to be shot by any one of the light-horse-men: *Provided*, That no person or persons shall suffer death for killing another in self-defence or by accident.

Approved November, 1834.

AN ACT for punishing infanticide.

SEC. 6. *Be it enacted, &c.*, That any person or persons

who shall be convicted of the crime of infanticide shall receive sixty lashes on the bare back.

Approved November 7, 1834.

An ACT forbidding compensation and making the person destroying the stock of another, where the fence is not lawful, liable to make restitution.

SEC. 7. *Be it enacted, &c.*, That no person or persons shall be allowed any compensation for any damage that he may sustain from stock breaking into his farm, unless his or her fence be made of good rails and ten rails high.

And be it further enacted, That if any one not having a lawful fence should destroy or injure the stock of another for breaking into his or her farm, he or she shall be liable to pay the value of the stock so injured or destroyed.

Approved November, 1834.

AN ACT pointing out the duty of the light-horse-men to visit every neighborhood twice a year.

SEC. 8. *Be it enacted, &c.*, That the light-horse-men of the several districts of the Choctaw Nation shall hereafter be required to visit all the neighborhoods within their respective districts at least twice in every year, and to advise the people to abstain from spirituous liquors, and to keep good order in their neighborhoods.

Approved November 8, 1834.

SESSION II.—1835.

AN ACT defining what constitutes lawful matrimony.

SEC. 1. *Be it enacted, &c.*, That the following mode of matrimony shall be lawful in this Nation: viz. the parties shall go before any captain or preacher of the gospel in the Nation, who shall ask the groom: "Are you willing to marry this woman whom you hold by the hand as your lawful wife?" if he says, yes, then the captain or the preacher of the gospel shall then ask the woman, "Are you willing to become the wife of this man who holds you by the hand?" if she says, yes, or be silent, he shall say, "I pronounce you man and wife:" *Provided*, All marriages previous to this act shall be valid and lawful, and all property shall upon the death of the husband descend to the wife and children of the deceased husband, and in case of the death of the wife the husband shall inherit the estate.

Approved October 8, 1835.

SESSION III.—1836.

AN ACT making the owners of hogs responsible for all damages where the fence is lawful.

SEC. 1. *Be it enacted, &c.*, That a fence of four inch cracks between each rail, for two and a half feet from the ground, shall be considered a lawful fence; and hogs breaking into a field having such a fence, the owner or owners of such hogs shall be responsible for all the damages sustained, and the Courts of the several districts shall have cognizance of such cases.

Approved October, 1836.

AN ACT prohibiting the teaching of slaves to read, write or sing without the consent of the owner.

SEC. 2. *Be it enacted, &c.*, That from and after the passage of this act, if any citizen of the United States, acting as a missionary or a preacher or whatever his occupation may be, is found to take an active part in favoring the principles and notions of the most fatal and destructive doctrines of abolitionism, he shall be compelled to leave the Nation and forever stay out of it.

And be it further enacted, That teaching slaves how to read, to write or to sing in meeting-houses or schools or in any open place, without the consent of the owner, or allowing them to sit at table with him shall be sufficient ground to convict persons of favoring the principles and notions of abolitionism.

Approved October 5, 1836.

AN ACT requiring the appointment of guardian to attend to the property of orphan children.

SEC. 3. *Be it enacted, &c.*, That in case of the death of the father or of both parents, possessed of property, there shall be a guardian appointed by the Court in their respective district; so that the property belonging to the orphan may not be mismanaged or wasted; and in case there should be a slave or slaves it shall be the duty of the guardian to hire the said slave or slaves to the highest bidder for the benefit of the orphans, and he shall keep a strict account of the nett proceeds of said property, and the Court shall allow the said guardian for his services a just compensation out of the estate. But should the widow be appointed, and should she get married and waste the said estate, the Court shall appoint another in her place.

Approved October, 1836.

AN ACT making the person who sets the woods on fire responsible for all damages done.

SEC. 4. *Be it enacted, &c.*, That if any person should be found setting the woods on fire, and if the fire should destroy any stock, fences or other articles of any person, and if the person or persons so injured shall be able to prove the fact against the offender, and shall inform the Court, the said Court shall decide on the case, and shall make allowance according to the value of said property, and cause the same to be paid by the offender to the person or persons so injured.

Approved October 5, 1836.

AN ACT prohibiting slaves from having property or arms, and making the owners amenable therefor.

SEC. 5. *Be it enacted, &c.*, That after two months from the passage of this act, that no negro slave shall be in possession of any property or arms. And slaves so offending shall forfeit all such property or arms as may be found in their possession, and said property shall be sold to the highest bidder by any of the light-horse-men, and the proceeds thereof be placed in the Choctaw funds.

Be it further enacted, That any master or mistress who shall protect slaves so offending shall be liable to pay ten dollars fine for each offence.

And be it further enacted, That any negro slave infringing on any of the Choctaw rights shall be driven out of company to behave himself; and if such offender should return and intrude any further, he shall receive ten lashes by the lignt-horse-men or any other person.

And be it further enacted, That any good honest slave shall be permitted to carry a gun by having a written pass from his master or mistress.

Approved October, 1836.

AN ACT allowing the Choctaws to intermarry without any regard to distinction as to *Iksa*.

Sec. 6. *Be it enacted*, *&c.*, That the custom of not intermarrying with their own Iksa among the Choctaw people shall forever be abolished; and all persons without any distinction of Iksa are left to make their own choice as to whom they shall marry.

Approved October 6, 1836.

AN ACT prohibiting the obstructing or shutting up of public roads.

Sec. 7. *Be it enacted*, *&c.*, That if any person or persons shall stop up or obstruct any public roads in any way whatever, either by throwing trees across them or by making fields over them, he or they shall pay a fine not exceeding one dollar, to be determined by the Court; except on condition that he or they shall remove the obstruction or make another road around said obstruction equally as good as the former; but should any other person or persons open such obstruction, he or they shall receive the fine.

Approved October, 1836.

AN ACT requiring white men who wish to work in the Nation to obtain a written permit from the Chief or the Agent; and also rendering any one hiring a whiteman without such permit liable for any depredation that such white man may commit.

SEC. 8. *Be it enacted, &c.*, That all white citizens of the United States, wishing to remain in the Nation under employ of any person, citizen of the Choctaw Nation, may do so by procuring permission in writing from the Chief or the United States Agent. But should any person, citizen of this Nation, receive any white man into his employ, not having the regular permission to remain in the Nation, and should such white man commit any depredation, or run away with any property belonging to the Nation, the person so employing shall pay all damages, and make good to the person or persons for property so stolen or injury sustained.

Approved October 8, 1836.

AN ACT requiring property stolen from citizens of the United States, or other tribes, to be returned.

SEC. 9. *Be it enacted, &c.*, That any property, of whatsoever nature it may be, stolen by any citizen of the Choctaw Nation, from any of the neighboring tribes of Indians or citizens of the United States, and brought into the Nation, said property shall be delivered to the District Chiefs, who shall inform the United States Agent of such offenders, and the property thus stolen shall be returned if possible to the proper owner or owners.

Approved October, 1836.

AN ACT providing that public iron and shops be for the exclusive benefit of the Nation.

SEC. 10. *Be it enacted, &c.*, That the public iron, steel and blacksmith shops furnished this Nation by treaty stipulations, shall not in any way whatever be used for the benefit of persons not citizens of this Nation, except in cases of great emergency; and all profits arising therefrom in each district shall be strictly accounted for and paid over to the district clerk and be as district funds.

Approved October, 1836.

AN ACT establishing the salary of the District Clerks.

SEC. 11. *Be it enacted, &c.*, That the salary of each District Clerk be fifty dollars per annum.

Approved October, 1836.

AN ACT preventing any Indian, not a Choctaw, to settle in the Nation without permission from the General Council.

SEC. 12. *Be it enacted, &c.*, That from and after the passage of this act no person belonging to any tribe of Indians or people, not a descendant of the Choctaws, shall be permitted to settle in the Nation, or purchase any improvement of any citizen or citizens of this Nation, unless by permission from the General Council.

Approved October, 1836.

AN ACT providing for the appointment of guardians for the minors residing out of the Nation.

SEC. 1. *Be it enacted, &c.*, That suitable guardians be appointed, who shall have the care of the persons and property of those Choctaw minors who are residing out of the Nation, and wish to remove to and reside therein.

SEC. 2. *Be it further enacted*, That the Judges of Courts in the respective districts have power to appoint all such guardians with the approbation of the United States Agent.

SEC. 3. *Be it further enacted*, That said guardians be required to give bonds, with approved security, in such penal sums as the Agent shall direct, for the faithful discharge of their duties; and all such bonds shall be lodged with the Agent.

SEC. 4. *Be it further enacted*, That said guardians shall make an inventory of all property of said minors committed to their care, and return such inventory to the Agent within a reasonable time after their appointment.

SEC. 5. *Be it further enacted*, That all such guardians be authorized to appear before the civil courts of the United States respectively wherein such minors dwell, and upon satisfactory evidence of their appointment, and of the wish of said minors to remove being furnished to the said court, the said guardians are authorized to take care of said minors and the charge of their property. And where guardians have already been appointed by the civil authorities in the States respectively, the guardians appointed according to the provisions of this statute may assume the responsibilities of the other guardians, in such way and manner as the courts of the States may provide for the greater safety of said minors and their property.

SESSION IV.—1837.

AN ACT for punishing the abusing or disfiguring of a horse running at large.

SEC. 1. *Be it enacted, &c.*, That any person taking up a horse out of the woods, knowing at the same time that the horse is not an estray, and abusing it by ill usage and disfiguring it by shaving its tail and mane, shall pay a fine not exceeding ten dollars, where the charges can be proved against him. In all such cases the courts shall determine the penalty.

Approved October 4, 1837.

AN ACT making it the duty of a man who runs away with a woman to marry her.

SEC. 2. *Be it enacted, &c.*, That when a man runs off with a woman he shall take her to the nearest captain and shall be married by the said captain, *Provided*, That he wishes to take her and keep her as a wife, and no person shall have the right to go and take that woman away from her husband when she wishes to live with him, and abusing her by beating her or by cutting off her hair. If any person should interfere with the couple the captain who married them shall advise them not to abuse her in any way whatever.

Approved October, 1837.

AN ACT respecting the pay of Indian doctors.

SEC. 3. *Be it enacted, &c.*, That no "sucking" or "conjuring" Indian doctor shall have the right to take any such property as horses, cattle, hogs or guns from any sick person who shall die under his care; nor from any person else unless he raises up the sick, then he shall be entitled to whatever shall be offered him; yet he shall have a right to take goods.

Approved October, 1837.

AN ACT making the money arising from the sales of strays to be District funds.

SEC. 4. *Be it enacted, &c.*, That all the money arising from the sales of strays shall be as District funds, and each District shall be entitled to the money raised from the strays in said District.

Approved October, 1837.

AN ACT laying a fine on those who sell whiskey, and also for the disposal of said fine.

SEC. 5. *Be it enacted, &c.*, That any person who shall bring whiskey into this Nation and shall sell to any person, shall pay such fine as the court shall determine; and the informer shall receive such pay out of the fine as the court shall adjudge; and the remaining sum shall be put in care of the clerk of the district as district funds. But should the offender not be able to raise the money, any one of the light-horsemen shall take such property as the offender may have in possession, and shall sell it, and pay the fine from the proceeds thereof.

Approved October 5, 1837.

[N. B. All the laws up to this are signed by Joseph Kincaid, Thomas Leflore and Nitakache, Chiefs.]

SESSION V.—1838.

AN ACT prohibiting any Choctaw citizen from cohabiting with a slave.

Sec. 1. *Be it enacted, &c.*, That from and after the passage of this act, that if any person or persons, citizens of this Nation shall take up with a negro slave, he or she so offending shall be liable to pay a fine not less than ten dollars nor exceeding twenty-five dollars, and shall be separated. And for the second offence of a similar nature the party shall receive not exceeding thirty-nine lashes nor less than five on the bare back, as the court may determine, and be separated.

Approved October, 1838.

By JOHN McKINNEY,
PIERRE JUZAN,
Chiefs.
GEORGE OKCHA̱YA,
Speaker.

AN ACT making any one who pulls or leaves down the fence of another liable to fine.

Sec. 2. *Be it enacted, &c.*, That any person or persons who shall be convicted of the crime or misdemeanor of pulling and leaving down any person's field or farm fence, shall be compelled to pay such fine as the court may estimate the damage done to the owner of the farm.

Approved October, 1838.

AN ACT providing for the separation of man and wife and for defining the compensation of performing marriage ceremony.

Sec. 3. *Be it enacted, &c.*, That if any person shall put away his wife or her husband without a sufficient cause shown to the court, such person shall be compelled to pay ten dollars; which money shall be placed in the charge of the district clerks or treasurer for public purposes; but in case the parties shall separate by mutual consent, neither of them shall be liable to a fine.

And be it further enacted, That persons authorized by law to perform marriage ceremony shall be paid for their services one dollar for every couple they shall join together.

Approved October, 1838.

AN ACT for the regular continuance of Courts in case of death or inability of any of the Judges.

SEC. 4. *Be it enacted*, *&c.*, That in case of death, or inability to act of any of the judges of the Supreme and Inferior courts in the several districts, any of the judges in the same district, on being notified, shall be obliged to preside and carry on the court when such vacancy happens until the Chief shall appoint another in his place.

Approved October, 1838.

AN ACT in relation to Salt Works.

SEC. 5. *Be it enacted*, *&c.*, That from and after the passage of this act, no person or persons shall be allowed to settle or destroy timber within half a mile of any salt works in this Nation, and all persons who shall settle within the above named distance from such salt works shall be liable to be removed by the light-horse-men of the district in which such salt works may be established, on application being made to the chief of the same, in case the person so settled will not remove voluntarily upon being notified of the passage of this act.

Approved October, 1838.

AN ACT defining the pay of the District Speakers.

SEC. 6. *Be it enacted*, *&c.*, That the Speakers in Mushulitubbi, Apakshanubbi and Pushimataha Districts shall be allowed fifty dollars per annum while they shall hold their office.

Approved October, 1838

SESSION VI.—1839.

AN ACT defining the place of holding elections for Chief and other officers of Pushimataha District.

SEC. 1. *Be it enacted, &c.*, That from and after the passage of this act the place of holding elections for Chief and other officers of Pushimataha District shall be changed from Lexington to Okayanulli, on the road leading from Fort Towson to the crossing of said Okayanulli.

Approved October 10, 1839.

—

AN ACT prohibiting any one from settling on improved lands within a specified distance.

SEC. 2. *Be it enacted, &c.*, That from and after the passage of this act, no citizen or citizens of this Nation shall be allowed to settle on improved lands within a shorter distance than four hundred and forty yards in a direct line from a former settler, without his or her consent. And any citizen so offending or violating this act shall be liable to pay a fine for damages to such an amount of money or property as a disinterested jury may determine; and such offender or offenders shall be compelled by the light-horse-men to remove out of the limits herein specified: *Provided*, Such settlement be not within an acknowledged town, place of gathering or village.

Approved October 11, 1839.

—

AN ACT for the punishment of traitors, and also for removing any white man who may advise the sale of the country.

SEC. 3. *Be it enacted, &c.*, That any chief, captain or citizen of this Nation who shall sign any instrument of writing in any way conveying or making sale of any portion or the whole of the Choctaw Nation, shall be deemed a traitor and an enemy to his country, and shall suffer death.

And be it further enacted, That any white man in this Nation, who shall advise or encourage any citizen of this Nation, verbally or in writing, to consent or agree to a sale of any part or the whole of this Nation, shall be deemed a bad man, and an enemy to the Choctaw people; and on application being made to the Agent or district chief in which such offender may be found, shall be forthwith ordered out of this Nation.

Approved October 9, 1839.

AN ACT giving power to Judges to direct light-horse-men to force criminals to attend court, and also for securing the attendance of witnesses at court.

SEC. 4. *Be it enacted, &c.*, That from and after the passage of this act, the Judges of the Supreme and Inferior courts of the several districts of this Nation, shall have full power to order and to direct the light-horse-men to bring to court any criminal or offender against the laws of this Nation. Any person or persons refusing to obey the summons of the officers aforesaid, by taking up arms or weapons against said officers shall be liable to be killed or taken by force of arms by maiming or otherwise, as the necessity of the case may be.

And be it further enacted, That if any important witness is summoned to attend court, and shall refuse to do so, he or she shall be liable to an action in court, and be made to pay a fine not less than ten dollars nor exceeding twenty dollars.

Approved October 12, 1839.

AN ACT giving power to the Judges to call Court every Wednesday.

SEC. 5. *Be it enacted, &c.*, That any Judge or Judges, who shall deem it necessary, shall have power to call court on every Wednesday throughout the year.

Approved October 12, 1839.

[The acts of Sessions V and VI were signed by John McKinney and Pierre Juzan, Chiefs, and George Okchaya, Speaker.]

SESSION VII.—1840.

AN ACT relative to the right of property in dispute, and also for paying light-horse-men and jury-men for their services in such cases.

SEC. 1. *Be it enacted, &c.*, That from and after the passage of this act, that when disputes arise between citizens of this Nation respecting the rights of property, and upon complaint being made to the chief or judges of the district in which such difficulty may exist, it shall be their duty to order the light-horse-men to seize and hold in custody such property until the court can be held and the rights of property be tried: *Provided however*, When the defendant can give good security in the presence of one or more light-horse-men for the forth-coming of such property in dispute at the ensuing court, he or she may be permitted to hold the same until the court shall decide; and in all cases where property is held in custody for trial, the party losing the suit shall pay the light-horse-men and jury for their services as may be determined by the court.

Approved October 7, 1840.

JAMES FLETCHER,
JOHN McKINNEY,
PIERRE JUZAN,
Chiefs.

AN ACT making it the duty of the light-horse-men to apprehend murderers and criminals.

Sec. 2. *Be it enacted*, &c., That all murderers and criminals in this Nation shall, by order of the chief or judge, be apprehended by the light-horse-men and held in confinement until they can be tried in the courts.

Approved October, 1840.

AN ACT to prevent false registries.

Sec. 3. *Be it enacted*, &c., That from and after the passage of this act, that any captain who shall knowingly register any person or persons living in another district, shall forfeit his own annuity, and this money shall go to the district funds in which the captain lives.

Approved October, 1840.

AN ACT prohibiting free negroes to reside in the Nation, and also making the employer liable to punishment, and further, making it the duty of the light-horse-men to take up negroes suspected free.

Sec. 4. *Be it enacted, &c.*, That by the first day of March next, 1841, all free negroes in this Nation, unconnected with the Choctaw and Chickasaw blood, are hereby ordered to leave this Nation, and forever to keep out of it, or they will be taken up and sold to the highest bidder, and made slaves for life.

And be it further enacted, That the captains of the light-horse-men in each district, where such sale or sales take place, are authorized to give a good bill of sale for each negro that may be sold.

And be it further enacted, That the money arising from such sales shall be divided, and each district receive its share, according to population, after paying light-horse-men for their services in taking and keeping such negro or negroes in custody until sold.

And be it further enacted, That all citizens of this Nation are debarred from hiring any free negro or negroes, or keeping them concealed or protecting them in any way whatever or manner whatever, in order to evade the true intent and meaning of this law, shall be subject to a fine not less than $250 nor exceeding $500; and if unable to pay the fine shall receive fifty lashes on the bare back.

And be it further enacted, That any white man in this Nation, who shall abet, encourage, or in any way whatever conceal a free negro, in order to screen them from the provisions of this law, shall be forthwith ordered out of this Nation by the Chief or the Agent. And where well founded suspicion rests that a negro is free, it shall be the duty of the light-horse-men to take such negro into custody, and in so doing if hostile resistance should be made, the light-horse-men or party so taking shall be at liberty to kill or maim as may seem expedient; and in all such cases the burthen of proof shall rest upon the negro or master to establish the fact of such negro or negroes being, *bona fide*, a slave: *Provided*, That William Black and Lewis Durant, Senior, be exempt from the operation of this law.

Approved October, 1840.

AN ACT making the pistols of the light-horse-men the property of the Nation.

Sec. 5. *Be it enacted, &c.*, That the pistols given to the Nation by the United States Government, for the use of the light-horse-men, be considered as public property, and in case of death or resignation the pistols shall be transferred to their successors in office.

Approved October 8, 1840.

AN ACT showing what is necessary for white men to marry in this Nation, and also laying a fine on those who perform marriage ceremony contrary to this act.

Sec. 6. *Be it enacted, &c.*, That no white man shall be allowed to marry in this Nation unless he has been a citizen of the same for two years.

And be it further enacted, That he shall be required to procure a license from some judge or the district clerk and be lawfully married by a minister of the gospel, or some other authorized person, before he shall be entitled and admitted to the privilege of citizenship.

And be it further enacted, Should any officer or minister of the gospel, who are authorized by law to marry in this Nation, perform such marriage ceremony not agreeable to this act, shall be made to pay a fine of one hundred dollars for each offence, and the money shall be put into the district treasury in which said marriage ceremony may have taken place.

And be it further enacted, That no white man who shall marry a Choctaw woman shall have the disposal of her property without her consent; and any white man parting from his wife, without just provocation, shall forfeit and pay over to his wife such sum or sums as may be adjudged to her by the district court for said breach of the marriage contract, and be deprived of citizenship.

Approved October, 1840.

—

AN ACT specifying the duties of the district clerks and judges with respect to keeping a record of the courts.

SEC. 7. *Be it enacted, &c.*, That from and after the passage of this act, each clerk of the several districts shall be furnished with a large blank book out of the district funds to keep a correct record of all the proceedings of the several courts in his own district.

And be it further enacted, That the judges in the several districts of each court shall furnish the district clerk in their respective districts with a full copy of all trials under his jurisdiction, with his name signed to it, which bill shall be filed and put on record.

Approved October, 1840.

—

AN ACT for the punishment of incendiaries and other destroyers of property and also of accessories.

SEC. 8. *Be it enacted, &c.*, That any person or persons who shall be convicted of the crime of burning another person's house or houses, or in any manner destroying the property belonging to a citizen of this Nation shall be subject to a fine equal to the value of the property so destroyed, and in addition, shall receive such corporeal punishment as the court may determine; but such punishment shall not exceed thirty-nine lashes on the bare back, unless such person be unable to pay the fine, in which case he, she or they shall receive one hundred lashes.

And be it further enacted, That accessories and advisors to such crime shall suffer half the burthen of the fine and punishment.

Approved October, 1840.

AN ACT providing for the apprehension and disposal of negroes suspected to be runaways.

SEC. 9. *Be it enacted, &c.*, That from and after the passage of this act, that it shall be the duty of any one in this Nation to take up a negro whom he may suspect as a runaway: *Provided, however*, That any person or persons who may apprehend a negro as a runaway, he shall give the owner, where he is known, information by the earliest opportunity. And if such negro be caught any distance less than twenty-five miles from home, the person so apprehending shall be entitled to five dollars; and if caught over that distance he shall receive ten dollars from the owner of said runaway negro.

And be it further enacted, &c., That it shall be the duty of the person so taking up a runaway negro to report to the district clerk of the district in which such runaway may be taken up. And it shall be the duty of the district clerk to record the description of said runaway on his book, and for every such service the clerk shall receive five dollars, and the person who may have apprehended and secured such runaway shall be entitled to one dollar and a half per day, for every day he may have him in custody.

And be it further enacted, That it shall be the duty of the clerk to advertise the same in one or more public places in each district in this Nation. And where it appears that such runaway is from any of the United States, it shall be the duty of the clerk to send an advertisement for publication to some newspaper editor in such State.

And be it further enacted, That if no owner appears in six months after the apprehension of said runaway negro, it shall be the duty of the light-horse-men to expose such runaway or runaways to public sale. And it shall be the duty of the captain of the light-horse-men to execute a bill of sale for such negro to the purchaser. And the proceeds thereof shall be used to pay the expenses of apprehending, securing and advertising such runaway, and if there remain a balance of the proceeds it shall be put into the district funds for public purposes.

Approved October 8, 1840.

AN ACT respecting $5,000 allowed by the Chickasaws in the treaty of 1837.

Sec. 10. *Be it enacted, &c.*, That the $5,000 allowed by the Chickasaws to the Choctaws for and in consideration of the privilege of settling in the Choctaw Nation, be and the same shall be stopped out of the general annuity for 1841, agreeable to the provision of the treaty concluded between the Choctaws and Chickasaws at Doaksville, in January, 1837.

And be it further enacted, That the said $5,000 shall remain in the hands of the Agent until appropriation thereof be made, and an order signed by each district chief for the amount due to their respective districts.

And be it enacted, That the Chiefs of this Nation be instructed to notify the Agent of the passage of this act, and request him to comply with the provisions of the same.

Approved October 9, 1840.

AN ACT making the mill when finished the property of the individual who furnished the materials.

Sec. 11. *Be it enacted, &c.*, That any citizen of this Nation who has furnished the materials to erect a mill shall be entitled to the exclusive privilege and right thereof, when completed, as his private property.

Approved October 9, 1840.

[The acts of Session VII were signed by James Fletcher, John McKinney and Pierre Juzan, Chiefs.]

SESSION VIII.—1841.

AN ACT for punishing Slander.

Sec. 1. *Be it enacted, &c.*, That any person or persons who shall slander or attempt to injure another's character shall be subject to a fine, and if unable to pay a fine, the offender shall receive such corporeal punishment as may be determined by twelve jurors, and the fine so paid shall go to the person or persons whose character has been injured.

Approved October, 1841.

JAMES FLETCHER,
JOHN McKINNEY,
ISAAC FOLSOM,
Chiefs.

AN ACT locating an Inferior Court in Pushimataha District.

SEC. 2. *Be it enacted, &c.*, That the Inferior Court held heretofore at Cold Spring be changed and held at Big Spring.

Approved October, 1841.

AN ACT for the punishment of false swearing in a Court of Justice.

SEC. 3. *Be it enacted, &c.*, That if any person or persons be convicted of false swearing, or making false statements in a court of justice, such offenders shall be fined not less than ten dollars nor exceeding one hundred dollars, and shall receive not less than five nor exceeding thirty-nine lashes on the bare back.

Approved October, 1841.

[The acts of Session VIII were signed by James Fletcher, John McKinney and Isaac Folsom, Chiefs.]

SESSION IX.—1842.

AN ACT providing for a system of public instruction in the Choctaw Nation.

SEC. 1. *Be it enacted, &c.*, That there shall be, and there are hereby established the following Institutions of learning: viz. Spencer Academy, Fort Coffee Academy, Koonsha Female Seminary, Janubbi Female Seminary, Chuwahla Female Seminary and Wheelock Female Seminary.

SEC. 2. The foregoing Institutions of learning shall be, and they are hereby located at the following places: viz. The

Spencer Academy at the point on the Military Road where the buildings are erecting under the direction of the Committee appointed in 1841, about nine miles north of Doaksville. The Male branch of Fort Coffee at Fort Coffee, in Mushulitubbi District. The Female branch of this Academy shall be located in the same vicinity, by a Committee who shall be appointed by the General Council for that purpose.* The Koonsha Female Seminary at such point in Pushimataha District as may be selected by a Committee who shall be appointed by the General Council for that purpose. The Chuwahla and Janubbi Female Seminaries at such points in Apakshanubbi District as may be selected by a Committee who shall be appointed by the General Council for that purpose. The Wheelock Female Seminary in Apakshanubbi District, at Wheelock.

Sec. 3. There shall be, and there is hereby appropriated the following sums for the annual support of these institutions respectively: To the Spencer Academy, the sum of six thousand dollars per annum, secured to the Nation for educational purposes under the treaty made at Washington City in 1825. To the Koonsha Female Seminary, three thousand dollars per annum, from the interests arising from the Chickasaw funds, agreeable to the treaty concluded at Doaksville in January, 1837. To the Wheelock Female Seminary, sixteen hundred dollars, per annum, from the same fund. To the Janubbi Female Seminary, sixteen hundred dollars, per annum, from the same fund. To the Chuwahla Female Seminary, sixteen hundred dollars, per annum, from the same fund. To the Fort Coffee Academy, six thousand dollars, per annum, from the same fund.

The above sums of money shall be paid over to the Superintendents of the several institutions, from time to time, as it is received from the United States. And the additional sum of three thousand dollars ont of the money arising from

* The Female branch of this Academy is called New Hope, at the old schoolhouse where Mr. Wilson formerly taught school, about one mile from the Choctaw Agency.

the sale of the fifty-four sections of land set apart in the treaty of 1820 for educational purposes, shall, with the consent of the United States be applied to the support of the Koonsha Female Seminary.

Sec. 4. There is granted to each institution mentioned in this act the use of as much land as may be needed for cultivation, pasturage, &c. And also the right to take from the public domain any timber, rock, stone coal, or other materials which may be required for the use of the institution or establishment.

Sec. 5. The Superintendents and Teachers in the several institutions, with their families, if they have any, shall be furnished house room and lodging, and shall board at the same table with the pupils; but shall not receive in addition thereto, on an average, a salary more than four hundred dollars, per annum, each.

Sec. 6. Instruction in Agriculture and the Mechanical Arts shall, in the Male Schools, be combined with the instruction in Letters; and in the Female Schools, in addition to Letters, the pupils shall be instructed in Housewifery and Sewing, &c.

Sec. 7. One tenth of all the pupils taught in these different schools shall be orphans: *Provided*, so many apply for admission.

Sec. 8. The Fort Coffee Academy under the conditions, limitations and restrictions rendered in this act, shall be placed under the direction and management of the Missionary Society of the Methodist Episcopal Church: *Provided*, said Society will contribute one thousand dollars, per annum, to the above named institution.

Sec. 9. The Koonsha Female Seminary and the Chuwahla Female Seminary, the Janubbi Female Seminary and the Wheelock Female Seminary, under the conditions, limitations and restrictions rendered in this act, shall be placed under the direction and management of the American Board of Commissioners for Foreign Missions: *Provided*, They will contribute, annually, to the above named institutions in proportion as the Methodist Episcopal Church is required to do.

Approved November, 1842.

JAMES FLETCHER,
ISAAC FOLSOM,
NATHANIEL FOLSOM,
Chiefs.

AN ACT providing for the attendance of light-horse-men at the Schools.

SEC. 2. *Be it enacted, &c.*, That there shall be a light-horse-man appointed to act at each of the public schools in this Nation, and to receive their appointments from the trustees and superintendents of the schools to which they shall respectively belong, and receive a salary, to be determined by the trustees and superintendents, and paid out of the school fund, and whose duties shall be specified by the trustees and superintendents.

Approved November, 1842.

AN ACT providing for the return of runaway children from the schools.

SEC. 3. *Be it enacted, &c.*, That when a student, who may have been placed in school under the school appropriation, shall leave the school without leave or permission, he shall be returned forthwith by his parents or guardians, or be brought back by the light-horse.

Approved November, 1842.

AN ACT providing for the removal of children on the appropriation in the school who are incapable of learning.

SEC. 4. *Be it enacted, &c.*, That when a student, upon a fair trial of two years, is found, from mental inability, incapable to learn or improve, such pupils shall, at the request of the trustees, be removed from the institution, and others selected to fill the vacancy.

Approved November, 1842.

AN ACT regulating the ages of those received on the appropriation; also prohibiting any one from having more than one child on the appropriation.

Sec. 5. *Be it enacted, &c.*, That the male students selected to fill the schools shall be from the age of ten to sixteen, and females from the age of eight to fourteen years.

And be it further enacted, That no family hereafter shall be allowed to put more than one child in public institutions of this Nation; but those that have already two children at said schools, they shall remain until they complete their education, and those that have more than two in shall be compelled to take them out immediately or pay the expenses to the institution.

Approved November, 1842.

AN ACT prohibiting the establishment of a trading house within three miles of any school.

Sec. 6. *Be it enacted, &c.*, That no person or persons shall be allowed to establish a store or trading house within three miles of any of the public schools.

Approved November, 1842.

AN ACT requiring the regulations of the public schools to be laid before the General Council.

Sec. 7. *Be it enacted, &c.*, That the rules and regulations of each public school shall be laid before the General Council for its approval.

Approved November, 1842.

AN ACT showing what kind of cases may be brought by appeal before the National Court; and also for the attendance of a light-horse-man.

Sec. 8. *Be it enacted, &c.*, That all cases to be tried in the National Court of this Nation shall be only such appeals as shall have been taken from any of the Supreme District Courts of this Nation. The evidence necessary to be furnished before the National Court for the prosecution of any suit in said court may be by written affidavits or verbal statements personally made in court as the case may be. No jurymen shall be required to try any cases brought before the National Court; but the judges alone shall be deemed sufficient to decide on all suits at law referred to said court. Any one of the light-horse-men shall be required to attend the National Court, and shall be subject to the order of the judge or judges of said court in the same manner as prescribed in the other courts of the Nation.

Approved November, 1842.

AN ACT providing for the payment of Captains, District Attornies and the Judges.

Sec. 9. *Be it enacted, &c.*, That the captains to be elected next July, as specified in the Constitution, shall each receive ten dollars for their services.

And be it further enacted, That the District Attornies, National Judge together with the Supreme and Inferior Judges in the several districts, shall each receive twenty-five dollars out of the National funds as a compensation for their services.

Approved November, 1842.

AN ACT prohibiting the cutting down of hickory and pecan trees for the nuts.

Sec. 10. *Be it enacted, &c.*, That no person or persons shall cut down hickory or pecan trees for the nuts in this Nation; and the persons so offending shall be liable to a fine of two dollars per tree, and one half of said fine shall go to the informer and the other half shall be as district funds.

Approved November, 1842.

AN ACT limiting the number of light-horse-men in Pushimataha and Mushulitubbi Districts; and also for increasing their pay.

Sec. 11. *Be it enacted, &c.*, That from and after the passage of this act, the Chiefs in Pushimataha and Mushulitubbi

Districts shall have the right to curtail the number of light-horse-men to six in their respective districts.

And be it further enacted, That the light-horse-men in the several districts shall hereafter each receive ten dollars per annum, in addition to their former pay.

And be it further enacted, That they shall be paid out of the National funds.

Approved November, 1842.

AN ACT regulating the pay of the Members of Council, Chiefs and Clerks for attending Council.

Sec. 12. *Be it enacted, &c.*, That from and after the passage of this act, that each member to the General Council together with the chiefs and clerks of the several districts shall receive twenty-five dollars as a compensation for their services to the General Council.

Approved November, 1842.

[The acts of Session IX were signed by James Fletcher, Isaac Folsom and Nathaniel Folsom, Chiefs.]

SESSION X.—1843.

AN ACT prohibiting the riding of a stray horse out of the Nation.

Sec. 1. *Be it enacted, &c.*, That from and after the passage of this act, no man shall ever be allowed to take or ride any stray horse beyond the limits of the Choctaw Nation; and any one so offending shall pay the value thereof to the Nation or to the owner of said stray if said stray, should be lost in any way, or should be taken from him by fraud.

Approved October, 1843.

JAMES FLETCHER,
ISAAC FOLSOM,
Chiefs.

AN ACT defining the place of holding Supreme Courts and Elections in Apakshanubbi District at Hohtak.

SEC. 2. *Be it enacted, &c.*, That the place of holding the Supreme Court and Elections in Apakshanubbi District shall be changed to near the Six Town school-house on Hohtak.

Approved October, 1843.

AN ACT for removing the Public Shop in Apakshanubbi District three miles east of Standing Pine.

SEC. 3. *Be it enacted, &c.*, That the Public Shop in Apakshanubbi District at Standing Pine shall be removed to Harris Frazier's place, about three miles from Standing Pine.

Approved October, 1843.

AN ACT establishing the Inferior Court in Mushulitubbi District, at Nanititekile.

SEC. 4. *Be it enacted, &c.*, That the Inferior Court in Mushulitubbi District, formerly held at the school-house near Pheasant Bluff, shall be changed to a place called Nanititekile, on the road leading from the Choctaw Agency crossing Big Sambois.

Approved October, 1843.

AN ACT defining the place of holding one of the Inferior Courts in Mushulitubbi District, at Yakni Achukma.

SEC. 5. *Be it enacted, &c.*, That the Inferior Court Ground at Buck Creek in Mushulitubbi District shall be removed to Yakni Achukma.

Approved October, 1843.

AN ACT for the punishment of assault and battery.

SEC. 6. *Be it enacted, &c.*, That from and after the passage of this act, if any person or persons should strike or otherwise injure another person without provocation, through malice, so that such injured person should lose any time from his business, the person so offending shall be liable to be sued in the courts of this Nation, and shall be subject to fine and be compelled to pay by the light-horse-men such fine as the jury may determine, which fine when collected shall be paid over to the person so maimed or injured.

Approved October, 1843.

AN ACT making it the duty of Captains to have Studs castrated in their Captaincy.

SEC. 7. *Be it enacted, &c.*, That it shall be the duty of the captains of the several districts of this Nation, to cause and to have all the studs castrated within their respective captaincies, except such as the owner may wish to keep as studs. And if any such studs should do any damage to a stock of horses of another person, the owner of such studs shall pay all damages sustained; and such cases shall be determined by the courts. All persons having studs and having been informed by the captains to have them castrated, and will not have it done, such studs running with any person's stock, shall be castrated by order of the captains.

Approved October, 1843.

AN ACT to prevent the harboring of runaway negroes.

SEC. 8. *Be it enacted, &c.*, That any person who shall be guilty of harboring a runaway negro or negroes, shall, upon conviction, be made to pay the owner in any sum as the case may be determined by any court having jurisdiction of the same.

Approved October, 1843.

AN ACT defining the times of holding the Supreme Courts in the several Districts.

SEC. 9. *Be it enacted, &c.*, That the Supreme Court of Mushulitubbi District shall be held on the following days: on the first Monday in January, April, August and November. In Apakshanubbi District on the second Monday in January, April, August and November. In Pushimataha

District on the third Monday in January, April, August and November; and in the Chickasaw District on the succeeding Monday after the Supreme Court held in Pushimataha District.

Approved October, 1843.

AN ACT providing for the payment of fines.

SEC. 10. *Be it enacted, &c.*, That from and after the passage of this act, that the Judges of the several districts of this Nation, shall have power to order light-horse-men to collect all fines that may be imposed by any court of this Nation according to law; *Provided*, he or she is not able to pay at the time, they shall have three months; then if not paid in that time, the Judge shall order the light-horse-men to seize on their property and sell it to the highest bidder to pay said fine.

Approved October, 1843.

AN ACT relating to all strays, and the duty of those that take up, Judge, District Clerk and light-horse-men, with respect thereto; and also the pay of District Clerk, and the one that takes up.

SEC. 11. *Be it enacted, &c.*, That from and after the passage of this act, that all stray property, the owner of which is not known, shall be taken and posted as follows: That when any person shall take up any stray horse or horses, he shall be required to give public notice; and if the owner of such stray does not appear within three months from the time that such beast was taken up, then the one that took up shall take such stray before any judge; then it shall be the duty of the judge to authorize two or more persons to appraise the same, and the description and value taken down in writing, and a copy of the description and valuation shall be furnished the district clerk; then it shall be the duty of the district clerk to have the same advertised in one or more public places in each district. And if the owner of such beast do not appear within twelve months, after which time the property shall be sold to the highest bidder by any light-horse-man, by first giving fifteen days notice of the sale; and one half of the proceeds shall go to the one that took up, then he shall pay the district clerk one dollar and a half, and the other half of the the proceeds shall go to the district in which such stray may be sold; but should the owner appear before the expiration of twelve months, and prove his or her property before any judge, he or she shall be entitled to the same by paying one dollar and a half each to the district clerk and the one that took up.

Sec. 2. That every person who shall take up stray cattle shall be required to give public notice of the same, and if the owner of which do not appear within six months from the time that such stray was taken up, then the one that took up shall notify any judge of such stray property; then it shall be the duty of the judge to authorize two or more persons to appraise the same, and also state the age, brand, mark and color in writing, and a copy of the same shall be furnished the district clerk; then it shall be the duty of the district clerk to advertise the same in one or more public places in his own district, and if the owner of such animal do not appear within twelve months, after which time the property shall be sold to the highest bidder by any light-horse-man by first giving fifteen days notice of the sale, and one half of the proceeds shall go to the one that took up; then he shall pay the district clerk one dollar per head, and the other half of the proceeds shall go to the district in which such sale may take place; but if the owner of such animal appear before the expiration of twelve months, and prove his or her property before any judge, he or she shall be entitled to the same, by paying twenty-five cents per head each to the district clerk and the one that took up.

Sec. 3. That every person who shall take up stray hogs or sheep shall be required to give public notice of such strays, and if the owner of said strays does not appear within six months from the time such stray property was taken up, then the one that took up shall notify any judge of such stray property, then it shall be the duty of the judge to authorize two or more persons to appraise the same and state color and ear mark of each stray in writing, and a copy of the same shall be furnished the district clerk, and whose duty it shall be to advertise the same in one or more public places in his own district. And if the owner of such property should not appear within twelve months, after which time the property shall be sold to the highest bidder by any one of the light-horse-men by first giving fifteen days notice of the sale, and one half of the proceeds shall go to the one that took up, then he shall pay the district clerk twenty-five cents per head; but should the owner appear before the expiration of the twelve months and prove his or her property before any judge, he or she shall be entitled to the same by paying twelve and a half cents per head each to the district clerk and the one that took up.

SEC. 4. That no person shall take up any stray unless the same be found on his or her plantation, or running with his or her stock.

SEC. 5. That every person who shall take up a stray horse or horses shall be required to take said strays to the stray pen at every Supreme Court in their respective districts, and keep them during the collection of the people.

SEC. 6. That every person who shall take up any stray animal, and abuse the said animal so as to cause its death, shall pay the value of the stray to the owner or to the district, as may be determined by any court having jurisdiction thereof.

SEC. 7. That every person who shall take up any stray animal should fail to take said stray to the stray pen the second time, any judge shall appoint some other person or persons to take charge of said stray.

Approved October, 1843.

AN ACT respecting stray pen at each Supreme Court Ground in the three districts.

SEC. 12. *Be it enacted, &c.*, That there shall be a stray

pen of four hundred rails and good bars made in each of the three districts, at their respective Supreme Court Grounds. Any person shall have the liberty of making the said pen, who shall be paid five dollars out of the funds arising from the sales of strays.

Approved October, 1843.

AN ACT providing blank books to the District Clerks for recording all stray property.

SEC. 13. *Be it enacted, &c.*, That each clerk shall be furnished a good blank book proper for recording all stray property in their respective districts.

Approved October, 1843.

AN ACT defining the time of holding elections in the several districts.

SEC. 14. *Be it enacted, &c.*, That all the elections in the several districts shall take place on the second Wednesday in July.

Approved October, 1843.

AN ACT providing for the pay of Jurymen.

SEC. 15. *Be it enacted, &c.*, That from and after the passage of this act, all jurymen, when summoned to try any case in suit, shall each receive twenty-five cents for their fees for each case, to be paid by the person losing such suit.

And be it further enacted, That the Judge or Judges of the Court in which such suit may be determined, shall order the light-horse-men to collect such fees, either in money or property, at a fair valuation, and pay the same over to said jurymen. But in case the person or persons losing suit should be unable to make immediate payment, he or she shall be indulged three months to make payment.

Approved October, 1843.

AN ACT requiring the Clerks and Judges, under obligation by oath, to do justice at elections.

SEC. 16. *Be it enacted, &c.*, That all clerks and judges of elections shall be bound by oath or affirmation to do justice according to law.

And be it enacted, That no person or persons shall be allowed to vote after the polling is closed.

Approved October, 1843.

AN ACT defining the duties of the District Treasurers and Auditors; and also in case of death or resignation making it the duty of the Chief to appoint successors.

SEC. 17. *Be it enacted, &c.*, That from and after the passage of this act, that it shall be the duty of the District Treasurer to receive and pay over all public funds on a warrant issued from the Auditor of the public accounts in their respective districts; and whose duty it shall be to keep a strict account of all monies received and the expenditure of the same, and make a full report annually to the General Council.

And be it further enacted, That the auditor of the public accounts shall not be allowed to issue his warrant in favour or against the treasurer only in consequence of an appropriation made by the General Council.

And be it further enacted, That it shall be the duty of the auditor of the public accounts to keep a strict account of all monies paid over to the treasurer, and the amount drawn from the treasury.

And be it further enacted, That in case of death, resignation or inability of the treasurer or auditor, the Chief shall appoint another to fill the vacancy until the next General Council.

And be it further enacted, That the treasurers and auditors shall each receive for their services two and a half cents on every one hundred dollars on all money placed in their hands.

Approved October, 1843.

AN ACT respecting the three months shops in the several districts, and also for the pay of the Smiths and Strikers, &c.

SEC. 18. *Be it enacted, &c.*, That each Smith shall receive forty dollars per month, and Striker twenty dollars, and find themselves; and that said shops be under the control of the Chiefs of their respective districts.

Be it further enacted, That there shall be seven hundred pounds of iron and one hundred pounds of steel furnished to each of the district shops.

And be it further enacted, That the different district shops shall commence to work some time in March, and when they commence business they shall end in precisely three months.

And be it further enacted, That each of the district chiefs shall have the power to let out contracts for furnishing the district shop, within their respective districts, with the quantity of iron and steel and black-smith tools as stipulated in the act authorizing said shops; and that such contracts will be let out to the lowest bidder. The person or persons taking such contracts will be required to give a bond and approved security for the faithful performance of such contracts, and such bonds sball be equal to the value of said contracts.

Approved October, 1843.

AN ACT for establishing the Armstrong Academy in Pushimataha District.

SEC. 19. *Be it enacted, &c.*, That the sum of twenty-nine hundred dollars out of the four thousand and two hundred dollars be set apart and annually appropriated to be expended under the direction of the American Indian Association, in Pushimataha District, to be called Armstrong Academy: *Provided*, said American Indian Association will contribute and furnish one thousand dollars annually to the support of said Institution.

Approved October, 1843.

AN ACT for establishing Neighborhood and Sabbath Schools in Apakshanubbi District.

SEC. 20. *Be it enacted, &c.*, That the sum of thirteen hundred dollars be set apart and annually appropriated for the support of neighborhood and sabbath schools in Apakshanubbi District as follows, namely: Three hundred dollars shall be expended in John Robinson's neighborhood to be conducted by the Methodist Missionary Board, the site of which shall be selected by P. P. Pitchlynn, Forbis Leflore, Basil L. Leflore and Rev. Mr. Steel. Three hundred dollars to be set apart and annually appropriated for the support of Norwalk School, which shall be conducted by the American Board of Commissioners for Foreign Missions. And Fifty dollars to each of the following Choctaw Sabbath Schools, namely, Kowaiillé, Walnut Grove, near James Harkins's; Oka Homa, near Capt. Hoyubbi's; Chickasawha, on Red River; Saktichaha, near Col. James Fletcher's; Chuwahla, near Edmund McKinney's; Kiamichi, near Capt. George Pusley's; Nashoba, near Capt. Wolf's; Glover's Fork, near Capt. Ishtaya's, near Janubbi; Fisk's near the Public Shop; Clear Creek School, near Aaron's; Yakni Achukma, near James Garland's; and Apehka, near Capt. Shoney's.

SEC. 21. That each of the Choctaw Sabbath Schools shall have the power to appoint their own trustees, whose duty it shall be to appoint the teachers, and adopt such measures as they may deem necessary for the advancement and promotion of their respective schools, and to report annually the condition of said schools to the General Council.

Approved October, 1843.

AN ACT regulating the number of pupils from Apakshanubbi District that shall enter the Armstrong Academy.

SEC. 22. *Be it enacted, &c.*, That as Apakshanubbi District has drawn thirteen hundred dollars out of the four thousand dollars for support of neighborhood and sabbath schools in said district, she shall only be entitled to the balance of her proportion of students that shall enter the Armstrong Academy according to population.

Approved October, 1843.

[The acts of Session X were signed by James Fletcher and Isaac Folsom, Chiefs.]

SESSION XI.—1844.

AN ACT authorizing Judges to preserve order in time of Court.

SEC. 1. *Be it enacted, &c.*, That from and after the passage of this act, that the Judges of this Nation shall have, and are hereby invested with full power to keep good order and regulations at their respective courts. Any person or persons who should come and threaten the life of any person at court, or treat the court with contempt while in session, shall be taken into custody by the light-horse-men and fined not exceeding fifty dollars, the same to be determined by the judges of the court; and if the offender be unable to pay the money the judge shall have the right to order the light-horsemen to take any property belonging to him, and sell it to the highest bidder, and pay the said fine. The money thus collected shall go to the district treasurer for the use of district purposes.

And be it further enacted, That any person or persons refusing to be taken into custody for any criminal offences or for contempt of court, and shall take up any unlawful weapons, the light-horse-men shall have the power to take them dead or alive, and they shall be protected by the laws of this Nation.

Approved October, 1844.

THOMAS LEFLORE,
NATHANIEL FOLSOM,
NITAKACHE,
ISAAC ALBERTSON,
Chiefs.

AN ACT for prohibiting trading with Slaves.

SEC. 2. *Be it enacted, &c.*, That from and after the passage of this act, if any citizen of this Nation is known to trade or carry on trafficking of any nature whatsoever with any negro slave belonging to this Nation, and the fact can be established, said offender shall be liable to an indictment in any court or courts of this Nation having jurisdiction thereof, and shall be made to pay a fine of five dollars; and the fine when collected, one half shall go to the treasury as district funds in which such transaction may take place, and the other half shall go to the informer: *Provided, however*, any citizen wishing to trade with any negro slave in this Nation may do so by the consent of the owner or by the negro having a written permit to that effect.

Approved October 18, 1844.

AN ACT for an Inferior Court at Victor's.

SEC. 3. *Be it enacted, &c.*, That from and after the passage of this act, an additional Inferior Court in Apakshanubbi District shall be established at Mr. Victor's to be called Victor's Court Ground.

Approved October, 1844.

AN ACT providing for the payment of the Supreme Judges for attending the National Court.

SEC. 4. *Be it enacted, &c.*, That from and after the passage of this act, that in addition to their annual salary the sum of twenty-five dollars shall be paid to the Supreme Judges for each and every time they shall act as associate judges in the National Court, or for each time they shall attend the General Council.

Approved October, 1844.

AN ACT appointing Board of Trustees for the Public Schools in the Nation.

SEC. 5. *Be it enacted, &c.*, That from and after the passage of this act, that P. P. Pitchlynn, George W. Harkins, Robert M. Jones and Thompson McKinney be and are hereby appointed Board of Trustees for all the Public Schools in this Nation, and they and their successors as Board of Trustees, shall each receive fifty dollars per annum for their services out of the public funds.

And be it further enacted, That the Board of Trustees shall select as promiscuously from among the people, and as impartially as possibly can be done, the pupils to be placed in the different institutions of learning in the Nation, and it shall be their duty to attend the public examinations of the school or schools in their respective districts, and report to the Council the state and conditions of the different institutions annually.

Approved October, 1844.

AN ACT requiring Board of Trustees to examine the accounts of the Public Schools.

SEC. 6. *Be it enacted, &c.*, That it shall be the duty of the Board of Trustees, collectively or separately, to examine the accounts of the Public Schools quarterly, or at such time as may be necessary, and if correct, to certify upon honour to the correctness of the same.

Approved October, 1844.

AN ACT providing for the erection of Horse Mills at Spencer Academy, Fort Coffee and Armstrong Academy.

SEC. 7. *Be it enacted, &c.*, That the mill-wright, provided for under the Treaty of Dancing Rabbit Creek, shall be employed to build a horse mill at Spencer Academy, Fort Coffee and Armstrong Academy, the materials to be furnished by each of said institutions, and the United States Agent be notified to employ a suitable mill-wright to carry on the work as early as practicable.

Approved October, 1844.

AN ACT for preventing free negroes from any share in the Annuity or Public Shops.

SEC. 8. *Be it enacted, &c.*, That no free negro, unconnected with Choctaw blood, shall ever be allowed to draw any money from the Choctaw Annuity.

And be it further enacted, That no free negro shall participate in any of the black-smith shops belonging to the Choctaw Nation.

Approved October, 1844.

[The acts of Session XI were signed by Thomas Leflore, Nitakache, Isaac Albertson and Nathaniel Folsom, Chiefs.]

SESSION XII.—1845.

AN ACT providing for filling a vacant Captaincy.

SEC. 1. *Be it enacted, &c.*, That from and after the passage of this act, when a Captain's office is vacated in any of the several districts, his Speaker shall exercise the duties of captain until the next election day, at which time another captain shall be elected to fill such vacancy, only by the qualified electors belonging to the same company so vacated, which captain when elected shall only serve out the unexpired time.

Approved October 4, 1845.

THOMAS LEFLORE,
NITAKACHE,
ISAAC ALBERTSON,
Chiefs.

AN ACT for placing Spencer Academy under the direction of the Assembly's Board, and for establishing the school at Norwalk.

SEC. 2. *Be it enacted, &c.*, That Spencer Academy shall be placed under the control and direction of the Assembly's Board: *Provided*, that Board will contribute two thousand dollars annually to the support of the Institution; to be conducted in the same manner, with the same privileges, restrictions and conditions provided in the school act entitled: "An Act providing for a system of Public Instruction in the Choctaw Nation," passed 29th of November, 1842. And it shall be the duty of the School Trustees to request Rev. Cyrus Kingsbury to correspond with the above Board upon the subject, and if they will accept the terms offered, to urge them to come and take charge of the Institution at the earliest time possible.

And be it further enacted, That the salary heretofore received by Mr. Rind shall be expended upon Norwalk School, to be under the control and management of the American Board of Commissioners for Foreign Missions: *Provided*, said Board will contribute the proportion to the support of the school as agreed upon in the general School Act of 1842.

Approved October 7, 1845.

AN ACT transferring the funds expended in the National Shop at Spencer Academy to Mushulitubbi District for two years.

SEC. 3. *Be it enacted, &c.*, That from and after the passage of this act, the funds that have been heretofore appropriated to the support of the National Shop at Spencer Academy shall be expended in Mushilitubbi District for the term of two years, and the authorities of said District shall have the power to determine where the said shop shall be established.

Approved October 7, 1845.

AN ACT defining the Inferior Court and Black Smith Shop in Apakshanubbi District at Kullikashaha.

SEC. 4. *Be it enacted, &c.*, That from and after the passage of this act, that the Inferior Court in Apakshanubbi District held at Janubbi, together with the three months' shop, shall be removed to Kullikashaha.

Approved October 8, 1845.

AN ACT defining the place of holding the Inferior Court in Pushimataha District at Tiaktalaya.

SEC. 5. *Be it enacted, &c.*, That from and after the passage of this act, that the Inferior Court in Pushimataha District held at Yunnushbok shall be removed to Tiaktalaya, near Hopakanubbi's.

Approved October 8, 1845.

AN ACT defining the Council Ground in the Chickasaw District at the Boiling Spring.

SEC. 6. *Be it enacted, &c.*, That from and after the passage of this act, the Council Ground in the Chickasaw District shall be removed to Boiling Spring in said District, where the Annuities will be paid annually, and all Councils for the management and disposition of the Chickasaw funds that may be held out of the Chickasaw District, and without the sanction of the Chief of the District, shall be null and void.

Approved October 8, 1845.

AN ACT defining the place of holding the Inferior Court in Apakshanubbi District, at French's meeting-house, near Willis J. Harkins's.

SEC. 7. *Be it enacted, &c.*, That from and after the passage of this act, that the Inferior Court in Apakshanubbi District held at Nakishtaya's old place shall be removed to French's meeting-house near Willis J. Harkins's.

Approved October 8, 1845.

AN ACT granting a short time to Criminals before execution.

SEC. 8. *Be it enacted, &c.*, That from and after the passage of this act, that when criminals in this Nation are sentenced to death, the judge, after consulting the wishes of the criminal as to the time when he would wish to be executed, shall set the time, not exceeding ten days after the judgment is passed, Sundays excepted. In the mean time the judge shall order the light-horse-men to keep him in close confinement till the day of execution.

Approved October 8, 1845.

AN ACT making the introducer or seller of whiskey liable to fine when damage is done.

SEC. 9. *Be it enacted, &c.*, That from and after the passage of this act, any person or persons who shall bring spirituous liquors into this Nation, and give or sell it to any person or persons, and any person or persons thereby be maimed or injured, the one who brought and gave or sold it shall be liable to an action in court, and be made to pay a fine not less than one dollar nor exceeding one hundred dollars, and the fine so paid shall one half go to the person so maimed or injured and the other half to the district in which such suit may be brought.

Approved October 9, 1845.

AN ACT defining the Black-Smith Shop in Apakshanubbi District at Olakintubbi's.

SEC. 10. *Be it enacted, &c.*, That from and after the passage of this act, that the three months shop in Apakshanubbi District at Filihkatubbi shall be removed to a Spring near Olakintubbi's.

Approved October 9, 1845.

AN ACT prohibiting the giving of any contracts from the several Literary Institutions in this Nation to Foreigners.

SEC. 11. *Be it enacted, &c.*, That from and after the passage of this act. that no contract or contracts, issued from the public institutions, shall be given to any person who is not a citizen of this Nation, when the same can be furnished by citizens of this Nation as low as can be done by citizens of the States.

And be it further enacted, That Major William Armstrong be informed of the existence of this act by the Chiefs of this Nation.

Approved October 10, 1845.

[The acts of Session XII were signed by Thomas Leflore, Nitakache and Isaac Albertson, Chiefs.]

SESSION XIII.—1846.

SEC. 1. *Be it enacted, &c.*, That every suit that may be brought before the Inferior Courts shall always be entered in the nearest court to where the matter in controversy may have taken place, unless by mutual consent of the parties concerned.

Bill proposed by G. W. Harkins.

Approved October 15, 1846.

THOMAS LEFLORE,
S. D. FISHER,
PETER FOLSOM,
JAMES McLAUGHLIN,
Chiefs.

SEC. 2. *Be it enacted, &c.*, That when an appeal is granted from an Inferior Court to the Supreme Court, and from the Supreme Court to the National Court, the judges of said courts shall designate the District and Court where the appeal is given to, while the Court is in session, and hand it over to a light-horse-man with instructions to go forthwith and hand it over to the Judge of said Court.

Bill proposed by G. W. Harkins.

Approved October 15, 1846.

SEC. 3. *Be it enacted, &c.*, That if any student in the public schools in this Nation shall run off and go home with his clothes, that were given to him at the institution, and the parents or guardian of such student should fail or neglect to send him or his clothes back in the time prescribed, he or they shall be made to pay the value thereof from the annuity of such students, and parents or guardians.

Approved October 15, 1846.

SEC. 4. *Be it enacted, &c.*, That the Board of Trustees of Public Schools in this Nation shall be elected every four years by the General Council.

Bill proposed by Jonathan Cogswell.

Approved October 15, 1846.

SEC. 5. *Be it enacted, &c.*, That no negro slave can be emancipated in this Nation, except by application or petition of the owner to the General Council, and *Provided also*, that it shall be made to appear to the Council the owner or owners, at the time of application, shall have no debt or debts outstanding against him or her, either in or out of this Nation. Then, and in that case, the General Council shall have the power to pass an act for the owner to emancipate his or her slave, which negro, after being freed, shall leave this Nation within thirty days after the passage of the act. And in case said free negro or negroes should return into this Nation afterwards, he, she, or they shall be subject to be taken by the light-horse-men and exposed to public sale for the term of five years; and the funds arising from such sale shall be used as National funds.

Approved October 15, 1846.

SEC. 6. *Be it enacted, &c.*, That from and after the passage of this act, no negroes from the United States, or neighboring tribes of Indians, will be allowed to come and remain in this Nation, under the pretence of hiring himself or themselves to work, no matter whether they have papers or not. And all negroes violating the provisions of this act, shall be taken up by the light-horse-men of the District where such offender may be found, and shall receive on the bare back, not less than one hundred lashes each.

And be it further enacted, That all property, goods or chattels found in his or their possession, shall be seized and sold at public sale, and one-third of the proceeds shall go to the light-horse-men and the balance thereof be applied to some beneficial purposes in the District: *Provided*, *however*, That the above bill shall not extend to negroes passing through the country, or such as may be hauling for citizens or merchants in this Nation.

Bill proposed by Robert Love.

Approved October 15, 1846.

SEC. 7. *Be it enacted, &c.*, That it shall be the duty of the Supreme Judges in the several districts to summon and empannel jurymen only from such citizens as reside in the district in which such court is held.

By G. W. Harkin.

Approved October 16, 1846.

SEC. 8. *Be it enacted, &c.*, That from and after the passage of this act, that any person or persons disturbing any religious devotions shall be taken up and presented before the judge by the light-horse-men, who is hereby authorized by law to fine them, but the fine shall not exceed five dollars for each person so offending, and the fine so collected shall belong to the district in which it may be collected.

Bill proposed by Robert Love.

Approved October 16, 1846.

SEC. 9. *Be it enacted, &c.*, That all witnesses summoned to attend court shall be allowed two cents per mile going and returning from court, and fifty cents per day whilst attending at court till discharged; to be collected by the light-horsemen off the person losing the suit, except in cases of murder, in which case the district shall pay the witnesses.

Approved October 16, 1846.

SEC. 10. *Be it enacted, &c.*, That all temporary Clerks at every election, in the several districts of this Nation, shall each receive one dollar per day out of the estray funds.

Proposed by Allen Carney.

Approved October 16, 1846.

SEC. 11. *Be it enacted, &c.*, That no person shall be appointed or elected Judge in this Nation unless he can read the English or Choctaw Language.

And be it further enacted, That the Inferior Judges from the passage of this act, shall each receive the additional sum of five dollars, to be paid out of any money in the District Treasury not otherwise appropriated.

Bill proposed by Cornelius McCurtain.

Approved October 16, 1846.

SEC. 12. *Be it enacted, &c.*, That the law passed in Session 9th, Sec. 8*, be amended so as to read thus: That when there is a charge or charges brought against any one under the employment of the different schools in this Nation, the person so accused shall have a fair and impartial trial by the Board of Trustees before he shall be removed from the Institution.

By Allen Carney.

Approved October 16, 1846.

SEC. 13. *Be it enacted, &c.*, That every person who shall be convicted of having forged, counterfeited, or falsely altered any Will, Deed of gift, Note, or Order, or any other instrument in which any valuble consideration may be in question, shall be guilty of Forgery, and shall be punished with not less than thirty-nine lashes, and fined not less than twenty-five, nor exceeding five hundred dollars.

Bill proposed by R. M. Jones.

Approved October 16, 1846.

SEC. 14. *Be it enacted, &c.*, That the law passed in Session 3, Sec. 2*, be so amended as to read thus: That any person who shall be convicted of the crime of committing rape or forcibly ravishing a woman or girl, shall receive one hundred lashes well laid on his bare back. And for the second offence of the same nature the offender shall suffer death. But in case of an attempt only, to ravish a woman or girl, the court shall determine the penalty; but the guilty person shall not receive more than thirty lashes on the bare back.

Approved October 16, 1846.

SEC. 15. *Be it enacted, &c.*, That from and after the pas-

* The Sections here referred to in Session 9th and Session 3d are omitted.

sage of this act, the Inferior Court in Apakshanubbi District formerly held at Coddle's old shop, near Doaksville, is hereby repealed, and be changed to Hacher's on the new Military Road.

Proposed by John Robinson.
Approved October 16, 1846.

SEC. 16. *Be it enacted, &c.*, That after the expiration of twelve months from the passage of this act, all stray cattle in this Nation, two years old and above that age, and found to be without mark or brand, shall be taken or gathered by any person, and delivered to the Supreme Court, during the session of said Court, in the District where such property may be found. And if not claimed and proved by any owner of such property, it shall be sold to the highest bidder by the light-horse-men; and one half of the proceeds thereof be placed with the district funds for public purposes, and the other half shall go to the person who caused the same to be sold.

Proposed by Zedoc Harrison.
Approved October 16, 1846.

SEC. 17. *Be it enacted, &c.*, That from and after the passage of this act, no person or persons shall be allowed to drive horses, mules, cattle, hogs, or sheep from the range to which the same may belong. But it shall be the duty of every person or persons who may be driving horses, mules, cattle, hogs, or sheep, if any such stocks, not belonging to his or her drove, should join the drove, he or she who may be driving, shall halt the drove at the nearest pen or some other convenient place, and separate all such stock as do not belong to his or her drove, or the person or persons for whom they may be employed to collect or drive stock.

And be it further enacted, That if any person or persons shall violate the provisions of this act, shall pay a fine and damages according to the decision of the district court where such offence may be committed, for the use and benefit of the person or persons sueing for the same. And if any slave or slaves, employed in driving stock, should violate the foregoing provisions of this act, his or their owner or employer shall be liable to pay a fine and damages, according to the provisions of this act.

Proposed by Forbis Leflore.

Approved October 16, 1846.

Sec. 18. *Be it enacted, &c.*, That there shall be an Inferior Court established in Pushimataha District, to be held at or near Armstrong's place, on Jack's Fork.

Bill proposed by Jonathan Cogswell.

Approved October 17, 1846.

Sec. 19. *Be it enacted, &c.*, That after the passage of this act, there shall be one three month's shop established at Capt. John Robinson's.

Bill proposed by Forbis Leflore.

Approved October 17, 1846.

Sec. 20. *Be it enacted, &c.*, That all witnesses who are summoned to attend court and cannot go in case he is sick or his family, and gives good lawful excuse, he, she, or they will be required to give their statement under oaths before any acting judge, and the said judge shall take his or her statement in writing, which shall answer the same as if it had been made in court.

By G. W. Harkin.

Approved October 17, 1846.

Sec. 21. *Be it enacted, &c.*, That from and after the passage of this act, the District Attornies of the several districts of this Nation, shall be elected every year by the qualified electors within their respective districts, whose duties shall be to report all offences against the laws of this Nation to the judge in his district, and to prosecute them to the best of his abilities. Bill proposed by Jonathan Cogswell.

Approved October 17, 1846.

[The acts of Session XIII were signed by Thomas Leflore, S. D. Fisher, Peter Folsom and James McLaughlin, Chiefs.]

APPENDIX.

SESSION IV.—1837.

AN ACT appointing Delegates to Washington City, and making appropriations to defray the expense.

SEC. 1. *Be it enacted, &c.*, That fifteen hundred dollars out of the ensuing Annuity of this Nation, shall be appropriated as a compensation for the services of a Delegation to Washington City.

And be it further enacted, That the Executives of the General Council of this Nation shall give an order for said appropriation to the United States Agent, for said sum to be paid to such persons as the General Council may appoint for said purposes.

SEC. 2. *Be it enacted, &c.*, That a Delegation of three persons shall be commissioned to visit Washington City, whose duty it shall be to present the wishes of the Choctaws to the President and Congress of the United States; *Provided*, that these Delegates shall not have the right to present any thing to the President and Congress of the United States nor transact any business whatever contrary to the wishes of the Choctaws. And should they do it, it shall be null and void.

Be it further enacted, That if any one of these Delegates that the Council shall appoint should not be willing to visit Washington City, or should fail to go in consequence of death or sickness, the Chief of the District in which the member shall fail, shall have the power to appoint any other person in his stead, that he may think proper.

SEC. 3. *Be it enacted, &c.*, That Messrs. George W. Harkins, Pierre Juzan and Robert M. Jones be, and are hereby appointed and instructed to visit Washington City, as Delegates to present the wishes of the Choctaws to the President and Congress of the United States.

Approved October, 1837.

AN ACT locating the General Council House.

SEC. 2. *Be it enacted, &c.*, That the General Council House of the Choctaw Nation shall be built about half a mile West of Vaughn Brashear's Stand, on Kiamichi, on a hill near the road leading from Fort Smith to Fort Towson, selected by the unanimous consent of the members of the General Council.

Approved October, 1837.

[The foregoing acts were signed by Joseph Kincaid, Thomas Leflore and Nitakache, Chiefs.]

SESSION V.—1838.

AN ACT authorizing V. Brashear to keep the General Council House.

SEC. 1. *Be it enacted, &c.*, That Vaughn Brashear is hereby employed to take charge of the Council House at Nanihwaiya, in consideration of twelve dollars per annum.

And be it further enacted, That he is to keep the house clean.

Approved October, 1838.

[The foregoing act was signed by John McKinney, Pierre Juzan and George Okchaya, Chiefs.]

SESSION VII.—1840.

AN ACT for removing scattering bands of Indian tribes in the Nation.

Whereas, the United States have been called upon by the General Council of this Nation, agreeable to the stipulations of the Treaty made between the United States and our People, at Dancing Rabbit Creek, they having promised to protect us, and having failed their promise as stipulated in the Treaty, by neglecting to remove scattering bands of Indians, driven from Texas and elsewhere, who are now settling in our country and committing depredations on our citizens, by stealing horses, negroes, and other property, Therefore,

SEC. 1. *Be it enacted, &c.*, That the Chiefs of the several Districts of this Nation, shall have power to notify those tribes, by the light-horse-men, to leave the country by the first day of March next, 1841; and at the same time to give them to understand that if they refuse to obey on their part, it will be attended with serious consequences, as the Choctaws would be under the necessity of removing them by force of arms.

And be it further enacted, That in case those tribes refuse to leave the country, after due notice has been given them, that it shall be the duty of the District Chiefs to call out five hundred fighting men agreeable to the laws provided in such cases, namely: Apakshanubbi District shall furnish two hundred warriors; Mushulitubbi District, one hundred; Pushimataha District, one hundred; and the Chickasaw District, one hundred. And the three first to be subsisted and to be paid out of the Choctaw General fund for their services in expelling those intruders.

Approved October 9, 1840.

AN ACT for selling School Houses in Mushulitubbi District.

SEC. 2. *Be it enacted, &c.*, That the Public School Houses in Mushulitubbi District, namely: one at Pleasant Spring and one near Col. McKinney's shall be sold to the highest bidder, and the proceeds thereof shall be placed in the hands of the District Clerk as District funds.

Approved October, 1840.

AN ACT requiring the United States Agent to furnish a qualified Mill Wright agreeable to the Treaty stipulation.

SEC. 3. *Be it enacted, &c.*, That the three Chiefs of the Choctaw Nation be, and the same are hereby requested to call upon the United States Agent, Major William Armstrong, to furnish our Nation with a qualified Mill Wright, as early as practicable, agreeable to the provision of the 20th Article of the Treaty made and concluded with our people at Dancing Rabbit Creek.

And be it further enacted, That said Mill Wright shall commence his labor in whichever district an individual may be ready with the materials for the work, and as often as he shall complete one job in one district, he shall proceed to another district and commence his labour wherever the materials are ready, otherwise he shall continue his labour wherever the materials are furnished.

Approved October, 1840.

[The foregoing acts were signed by James Fletcher, John McKinney and Pierre Juzan, Chiefs.]

SESSION VIII.—1841.

RESOLUTIONS respecting the Choctaw Academy in Kentucky.

Whereas, we have strong assurance from recent information obtained through the War Department, that the wishes of the Choctaw people, so long disregarded in relation to the application of their educational funds, which are now expended in Kentucky, will be attended to; and we fondly hope very soon to see an Institution for the education of the rising generation located within our own Nation: We view this as an object paramount to all others, and the only efficient mode to advance our people; and we feel the obligation that devolves upon us to lay the foundation of this Institution upon a broad and solid basis, and we cannot but express our satisfaction at this change, Therefore,

SEC. 1 *Resolved, &c.*, That we will give a hearty co-operation to the location of this School within our own country, founded upon the resources of our Nation, as provided for in the Treaty stipulation, and so far as this, and all other educational funds belonging to the Nation, be placed under the control of the General Council, as far as may be compatible with existing Treaties.

SEC. 2. *Resolved, &c.*, That for several years we have looked upon the Academy in Kentucky as an institution not entitled to our patronage or confidence. In support of this it is only necessary to point to our youths who have returned to us uneducated with rarely an exception. Nevertheless, our funds have been expended there, and that too against our strong remonstrances. Our children now there have become restless, unhappy, and discontented, so as not to improve. We therefore wish them to return to us as speedily as possible.

SEC. 3. *Resolved, &c.*, That a sufficient sum of money, from the educational funds, be reserved and applied to the establishment and support of a School wholly designed for the education of the female children of our Nation, and that this School be located in the same manner as that for the male youths, after the arrangement for commencing the School for boys shall have been accomplished.

SEC. 4. *Resolved, &c.*, Until the next annual meeting of the Council, a Committee, consisting of two persons from each district, be appointed by this Council, who, with our Agent, be authorized and empowered with full authority to select a site for said School and to submit a plan for the erection of the necessary buildings, and to do all acts aud exercise all authority with which this Council shall clothe them to carry out the object designed by this resolution, until the next General Council shall adopt such further regulations and laws as may be right and proper.

SEC. 5. *Resolved, &c.*, That when the proper plan for the buildings and estimate of the cost thereof, shall have been made out, that our Agent be directed to communicate the same to the War Department for approval with a request for the transmission of funds necessary to meet the progressive expenditure.

SEC. 6 *Resolved, &c.*, That it is the wish and just expecation of this Council that in selecting a site for said Institution of learning, that the Committee to whom this responsibility and delicate duty shall be intrusted will divest themselves of all local and sectional prejudices, and in all things consult the true interests of the whole Choctaw Nation and of the Chickasaw people, the latter of whom unite in this resolution, and expect that the funds now appropriated for educating their youths in Kentucky be blended with the Institution designed to be established within the Choctaw country.

Sec. 7. *Resolved, &c.*, That the Committee be and are hereby required to keep a fair and legible record of their proceedings and submit the same to the next annual Council, and that a majority of said Committee shall be competent to transact the business confided to them.

Sec. 8. *Resolved, &c.*, That this Council address a letter to the Secretary of War in relation to the School in Kentucky, expressive of the feelings and wishes of this Council to bring that School to a final close on the first day of April, 1842; and that Col. P. P. Pitchlynn be appointed to proceed to Washington City with the said letter to the Department, more fully to explain our views and wishes.

Approved October, 1841.

AN ACT making appropriation for the payment of Black-Smiths.

Sec. 2. *Be it enacted, &c.*, That the sum of four hundred and eighty dollars be appropriated, out of the National funds, to pay Jackson Frazier the sum of two hundred and forty dollars, for his services one year in the Nationaal Shop at Nanihwaiya; and also the sum of two hundred and forty dollars to Harris Frazier, for services of Jesse McKinney's negro in the shop one year.

Approved October, 1841.

AN ACT making appropriation for the payment of Delegates to Creek Council.

Sec. 3. *Be it enacted, &c.*, That the sum of one hundred and forty dollars be appropriated to pay Joel H. Nail, Jerry Folsom, Okchaya and Swaney Frazier, from Apakshanubbi District; and Chief Isaac Folsom, Norman David Wall, James McCoy and Solomon from Pushimataha District; and also Chief John McKinney, William Riddle, Stephen Holsen and Lewis Calvin; and that the above appropriation be equally divided among them for their services to Creek Council.

And be it further enacted, That the sum of $12 25 taken from Pushimataha District by the men of Apakshanubbi District, for their expenses to the Creek Council, shall not be refunded or included in the above appropriation.

Approved October, 1841.

AN ACT respecting Thomas Wall's claim; and also the Nation's claim against the United States.

Sec. 4. Whereas, Thomas Wall, a citizen of this Nation, having laid a claim on Fort Smith, some years ago, after the evacuation of said Fort by the Government, and considered it to be his improvement, and being dispossessed by the erection of a new Fort at said Fort Smith, that he be entitled to such pay as the Government will allow for the old improvement at Fort Smith, Therefore,

Resolved, *&c.*, That Col. P. P. Pitchlynn shall be, and is hereby appointed and authorized to keep up a friendly correspondence with the Department of War, and with such other officers of the United States as he may deem expedient, upon the subject of all just claims which this Nation has against the United States Government, and to report the same to the Chiefs and General Council; but for such services said Pitchlynn shall not receive any additional compensation to that granted him by an act passed this day in Council.

Approved October, 1841.

AN ACT respecting $7,000, the Interest of the Chickasaw funds, granted to the Choctaws in the Treaty of 1837.

Sec. 5. *Be it enacted*, *&c.*, That seven thousand dollars of the interests arising from the funds granted to the Choctaws by the Chickasaws, is hereby reserved from the General Annuity of this year, and out of which the National debts shall be paid, together with the pay and salaries of the officers of this Nation; after which the residue of said seven thousand dollars shall be paid over to the District Treasurers in proportion to the population in each District.

And be it further enacted, That the Chiefs of this Nation are required to inform the Agent of the existence of this Act, and request him to reserve the funds as above specified.

Approved October, 1841.

AN ACT providing for the pay of Chaplain and Sergeant at Arms.

SEC. 6. *Be it enacted, &c.*, That the sum of eighteen dollars be appropriated out of the National funds as a salary for the Chaplain to the General Council of this year.

And be it further enacted, That the Sergeant at Arms who has attended to the Council shall be, and is hereby allowed eighteen dollars for his services.

Approved October, 1841.

AN ACT permitting Mrs. Ward and family and John and William Cooper to remain in the Nation.

SEC. 7. *Be it enacted, &c.*, That Mrs. Ward and family and William Cooper and John Cooper are hereby permitted to remain in the Nation during good behaviour.

Approved October, 1841.

AN ACT respecting forty youths to be educated in the United States.

SEC. 8. *Be it enacted, &c.*, That the forty youths to be educated, under provisions granted in the Treaty of Dancing Rabbit Creek, shall be sent with the consent of the President of the United States, out of the Nation, and be placed in four separate institutions of learning in the United States, viz: Ten Male youths in the Ohio University, Ten Male youths in Jefferson College in Cannonsburgh, Pennsylvania, and Ten Male youths in Asbury University, at Green Castle, Indiana.

Approved October, 1841.

[The foregoing acts were signed by James Fletcher, John McKinney and Isaac Folsom, Chiefs.]

SESSION IX.—1842.

AN ACT making appropriation for the payment of Delegate to Washington City.

SEC. 1. *Be it enacted, &c.*, That the sum of five hundred dollars shall be, and is hereby appropriated out of the National funds of this Nation, to defray the expenses of Col. P. P. Pitchlynn in going and returning from Washington City as Delegate from this Nation to attend to the public affairs of the Choctaw people.

Approved November, 1842.

AN ACT making appropriation of the seven thousand dollars, the interest money of the Chickasaw funds.

SEC. 2. *Be it enacted, &c.*, That the following sums of money are hereby appropriated and set apart of the seven thousand dollars formerly specified by a law, arising from the Chickasaw interest fund, to defray the current expenses of our Nation up to the end of the present year.

For Smiths, Strikers, Iron and Steel,	$4287 00
" Captains,	600 00
" Light-horse-men,	550 00
" Judges,	310 00
" Chiefs, Speakers and Clerks,	425 00
" Councilmen,	550 00
" Attornies,	75 00
" Delegates to Creek Council,	92 00
" the expenses of getting Smith	111 00
	$7000 00

And be it further enacted, That the Chiefs will inform Major Armstrong to reserve seven thousand dollars for defraying and paying the National debt, together with a copy of this to be furnished the Agent.

Approved November, 1842.

AN ACT for securing the right and privilege to Jonathan Cogswell to translate and print the Constitution and Laws of the Choctaw Nation.

SEC. 3. *Be it enacted, &c.*, That the exclusive right and privilege, for the term of eight years, is hereby secured to Jonathan Cogswell to translate and print the Constitution and Laws of the Choctaw Nation, both in the English and Choctaw language.

And be it further enacted, That if any person or persons translate or print the Constitution and Laws of this Nation before the expiration of eight years from this date, such person or persons so offending shall be liable to be prosecuted in any court of this Nation, and fined not less than one hundred dollars nor exceeding five hundred dollars.

Approved November, 1842.

SESSION X.—1843.

AN ACT for appointing Committee to locate the Female Seminary in Pushimataha District.

SEC. 1. *Be it enacted, &c.*, That Iacha-hopaiyi, William McCoy, Benjamin Brashears and Rev. C. Kingsbury are hereby appointed and authorized to act together as Committee, in selecting the site for the Female Seminary in Pushimataha District.

And be it further enacted, That such selection be made as quick as possible, so that said institution may get early into operation.

And be it further enacted, That in case they cannot agree, the District Chief shall have power to appoint another Committee to locate said site.

Approved October, 1843.

AN ACT for appointing Committee to locate the Chuwahla Female Seminary in Apakshânubbi District.

SEC. 2. *Be it enacted, &c.*, That John Frazier, William Bohanan, Forbis Leflore and Rev. C. Kingsbury are hereby appointed and authorized to select the site for the Chuwahla Female Seminary, and in case they cannot agree, the District Chief shall have power to appoint another Committee to locate said site.

Approved October, 1843.

RESOLUTION respecting Foreign Trade.

SEC. 3 *Resolved, &c.*, That the District Chiefs are hereby requested to write to the United States Agent, Capt. William Armstrong, and inform him that the citizens of Texas still continue to bring produce and stock into our country for sale, greatly to the injury and prejudice of our own citizens. And that our Chiefs be further instructed to ascertain if it be not in the power of the United States to protect us from such foreign trade; and also, if our General Council have not a right to pass laws to tax such produce and stock brought from Texas. And that if it be not in the power of our Council to pass those collecting laws, that our Chiefs be instructed to ask the Government, through the Agent, to send into our country a collecting officer, to collect duties of the citizens of Texas.

Approved October, 1843.

AN ACT providing for the pay of Creek Delegates.

SEC. 4. *Be it enacted, &c.*, That each of the Delegates to the Creek Council from Mushilitubbi District shall receive eight dollars, and each of those from Pushimataha District shall receive five dollars.

And be it further enacted, That ten dollars shall be refunded to Pushimataha District out of the National funds, which sum having been borrowed by said Delegates.

And be it further enacted, That the Chiefs in future shall not appoint more than two Delegates besides himself from each district.

Approved October, 1843.

[The foregoing acts were signed by James Fletcher, Isaac Folsom and Nathaniel Folsom, Chiefs.]

SESSION XI.—1844.

APPROPRIATION Bill.

SEC. 1. *Resolved, &c.*, That our Agent, William Armstrong, be, and is hereby authorized to pay the following sums for School purposes, from the investment on Alabama Bonds; which sums will be a payment up to the first of January, 1845. And thereafter the several teachers will be paid regularly semi-annually, commencing on the first of January, 1845.

To Rev. W. H. Goode, for Fort Coffee, from 1st of April, 1844, when last paid, to the 1st of January, 1845, 9 months, at $6000,	$4,500 00
To Rev. A. Wright, for Wheelock, from 1st of November to 1st January, 2 months, at $1,600,	266 66
To Rev. C. Kingsbury, for Chuwahla, from 1st September to the 1st of January, 4 months, at $1,600,	533 33
To Rev. E. Hotchkin, for Koonsha, from the 1st of May, the time he commenced, to the 1st of January, 1845, 8 months, at $3,000,	2,000 00
To Rev. C. Byington, for Janubbi, from the 1st of January, 1844, to the 1st of January, 1845, 12 months, at $1,600,	1,600 00
To Rev. R. D. Potts, for Armstrong Academy, up to the 1st of January, 1845,	2,900 00
For Neighborhood and Sabbath Schools, in Apakshanubbi District,	1,200 00
	$13,000 00

Approved October, 1844.

AN ACT for appointing Committee to select the site for the Armstrong Academy.

SEC. 2. *Be it enacted, &c.*, That the site for the Armstrong Academy shall be selected as early as practicable, by a Committee composed of the following persons, or such of them as will attend to their appointment.

Rev. R. D. Potts, Capt. Silas D. Fisher, Iacha-hopaiyi, Nicholas Cochneur, Isaac Leflore and R. M. Jones; and in case they cannot agree, they shall have power to appoint one or more persons to act in conjunction with them to select the site.

Approved October, 1844.

AN ACT making appropriation for the pay of Adam Nail.

SEC. 3. *Be it enacted, &c.*, That the sum of fifteen dollars shall be paid to Adam Nail, for his services rendered in attending the National Council as Supreme Judge of Mushulitubbi District.

Approved October 8, 1844.

AN ACT making appropriation for the pay of Nakishtaya.

SEC. 4. *Be it enacted, &c.*, That the sum of ten dollars is hereby appropriated to pay Nakishtaya for services rendered to Apakshanubbi District.

Approved October 9, 1844.

RESOLUTION requesting William McCoy to refund the $31 00 to the District.

SEC. 5. *Be it enacted, &c.*, That Mr. McCoy is hereby requested to pay the thirty-one dollars back to the District, as it was misplaced while in his possession, and that another Treasurer be elected for that District.

Approved October, 1844.

AN ACT making appropriation for the pay of Claimants.

SEC. 6. *Be it enacted, &c.*, That the sum of two dollars is hereby appropriated to pay Isaac Chukmubbi and Charles Campbell for services rendered in hauling of Public Iron.

Approved October, 1844.

AN ACT making appropriation for the pay of Mr. Cochran.

SEC. 7. *Be it enacted, &c.*, That the sum of eight dollars be appropriated to pay Mr. Cochran for the use of his house two years as Senate chamber, out of the District funds of the several districts.

Approved October, 1844.

A RESOLUTION requiring the Agent to take the necessary steps for removing Judge Doak from the Nation.

SEC. 8. *Resolved, &c.*, That Judge Doak shall leave the Choctaw Nation after a due notification of the passage of this resolution, and the Chiefs are hereby requested to inform Major William Armstrong, United States Agent, of the existence of this resolution, and request him to withdraw his license, and cause him to leave the Choctaw Nation.

Approved October, 1844.

AN ACT providing for the removal of some Indians in the Nation.

SEC. 9. *Be it enacted, &c.*, That all the intruding tribes of Indians that are now residing within the limits of the Choctaw Nation, shall be required to leave the Nation as soon as practicable. And that the Chiefs of this Nation be required to inform Major William Armstrong, United States Agent, of the existence of this Act, and request him to have them removed without the limits of the Choctaw Nation: *Provided, however*, The Cadoes, who at a previous Session of the General Council having obtained a permit to live in the Nation, shall be exempt from the operation of this Act; and also the following named families of Indians be allowed to remain unmolested by the operation of this Act, *viz*: Charley, Mike, McCoy, Cherokees; Little Boy and Frank's family and Strong Man, Delawares; Capt. Beaver, Panther and Oats, Shawnees, and their families; and one family of Quapaws living above the mouth of Washita, on Red River.

Approved October, 1844.

A RESOLUTION for tendering thanks to Major William Armstrong.

SEC. 10. *Resolved, &c.*, That the thanks of the General Council be tendered to Major William Armstrong, for the able and salutary advice which he has at all times freely given to the Choctaws, on all matters touching the vital interests of our people; and that the President of the Senate and Speaker of the House of Representatives sign this, and a copy of the same be sent to him.

Approved October, 1844.

A RESOLUTION authorizing the Clerks to have a fence made around the Council House.

SEC. 11. *Resolved, &c.*, That the District Clerks are hereby authorized and instructed to make a bargain with Mr. Cochran, or any other person, to put up a ten rail fence, and staked and ridered, of one acre of ground around the General Council House; also to shrub and trim the saplings and put up the gate: *Provided*, the same will not cost more than thirty dollars, to be paid out of the National funds of 1845.

Approved October, 1844.

A RESOLUTION respecting the Boundary Line of the Choctaw Nation.

SEC. 12. *Resolved, &c.*, That the Chiefs be requested to address a letter to Major William Armstrong, informing him of the state and condition of the boundary line separating our Nation from the State of Arkansas; and to request him to urge upon the Government the necessity of re-surveying and re-marking said boundary line.

Approved October, 1844.

AN ACT making appropriation for the payment of officers, for black-smithing, purchasing iron and steel and cotton cards, &c.

SEC. 13. *Be it enacted, &c.*, That the sum of thirty

hundred and sixty-four dollars and five cents be set apart and appropriated for the payment of the officers of this Nation, up to the year ending 1844. $3064 05

And be it further enacted, That the sum of thirty-four hundred and sixty-nine dollars be set apart and appropriated for the pay of black-smithing and for purchasing iron and steel for 1845, 3469 00

And be it further enacted, That the sum of three hundred dollars be appropriated for the pay of three School Trustees, viz: R. M. Jones, P. P. Pitchlynn and Thompson McKinney, up to the year ending 1844. 300 00

And that the sum of twenty-four dollars be appropriated to pay for cotton cards, used by Pushimataha District belonging to Berthelet, Heald & Co., 24 00

And the further sum of one hundred and forty-two dollars and ninety-five cents, which is the remaining balance of the seven thousand dollars, be, and the same is hereby set apart and appropriated to defray the expenses of black-smithing, &c., in Apakshanubbi District. 142 95

$7,000 00

Approved October, 1844.

AN ACT providing for the pay of Willis J. Harkins.

SEC. 14. *Be it enacted, &c.*, That the sum of thirty-five dollars is hereby appropriated to pay W. J. Harkins, for services rendered in hauling of public iron, and for the use of black-smith tools.

Approved October, 1844.

[The foregoing acts were signed by Thomas Leflore, Nitakache, Nathaniel Folsom and Isaac Albertson, Chiefs.]

SESSION XII.—1845.

A RESOLUTION providing for the safe keeping of the Patent from the United States.

SEC. 1. *Resolved, &c.*, That the Patent from the United

States Government for the Choctaw country, shall be placed in the hands of Col. Thomas Leflore for safe keeping.

Approved October 4, 1845.

AN ACT making appropriation of five dollars.

Sec. 2. *Resolved, &c.*, That the sum of five dollars be appropriated for one ream of paper for the General Council, and one dollar for the transportation of the same from Doaksville. The above to be paid for by the four Districts of this Nation.

Approved October 7, 1845.

A RESOLUTION tendering the thanks of the General Council to Dr. Simpson for gratuitous attendance on the Chuwahla Female School.

Sec. 3. *Resolved, &c.*, That the thanks of the Council be tendered to Doct. Simpson, Surgeon at Fort Towson, for his kind and gratuitous services rendered in attending the sick students at Chuwahla Female Seminary.

Approved October 7, 1845.

THOMAS LEFLORE,
NITAKACHE, *Chiefs.*
SLOAN LOVE, *Speaker.*

AN ACT requiring William Guthrie to leave the Choctaw Nation.

Sec. 4. *Be it enacted, &c.*, That William Guthrie, a trader, shall leave the Choctaw Nation after a due notification of this Act, and that the Chiefs are hereby requested to inform Capt. Armstrong, United States Agent, of the passage of this Act, and request him to withdraw his license, and cause him to leave the Choctaw Nation.

Approved October 8, 1845.

AN ACT providing for the pay of Creek Delegates.

Sec. 5. *Be it enacted, &c.*, That Nitakache, Poshishtikubbi and Jones Ponubbi shall be paid ten dollars each for their services in going to and returning from the Creek Council, in the spring of 1845.

Approved October 8, 1845.

A RESOLUTION providing for the payment of a Mill-Wright for building a Mill for Col. James Fletcher.

SEC. 6. *Be it enacted, &c.*, That the Chiefs be required to request Major William Armstrong to pay the Mill-Wright who built a Mill for James Fletcher, near Spencer Academy, out of the funds set apart in the Treaty of 1830 for the support of a Mill-Wright in the Choctaw Nation.

Approved October 8, 1845.

A RESOLUTION denying the right of the General Council to appropriate money from the National funds to defray expenses of the Chickasaw District.

SEC. 7. *Resolved*, That the General Council of the Choctaw Nation, assembled, have no right to appropriate out of their National funds to pay the current expenses of the Chickasaw District.

Approved October 9, 1845.

AN ACT providing for the payment of Benjamin Wright.

SEC. 8. *Be it enacted, &c.*, That Benjamin Wright be paid twenty-five dollars for working in the District Shop in Pushimataha District, half a month, in the year of 1844: *Provided*, there is no funds in the hands of the Agent retained from the pay of Mr. Balce, former smith, for that purpose.

Approved October 9, 1845.

AN ACT providing for the pay of Black Smith and Striker.

SEC. 9. *Be it enacted, &c.*, That Charles Milton be paid twenty dollars; also his Striker be paid ten dollars for their services in working in the black-smith shop at Janubbi, a half month, in the year 1843.

Approved October 9, 1845.

A RESOLUTION providing for the pay of Ponubbi.

SEC. 10. *Resolved* by the Joint Committee on Claims, That Ponubbi, of Pushimataha District, be paid twenty-five dollars, for hauling iron and steel from Doaksville, in the said District, for the different three months' shops.

Approved October 9, 1845.

A RESOLUTION providing for the pay of Swaney Frazier.

SEC. 11. *Resolved* by the joint Committee on Claims, That Swaney Frazier be paid twenty dollars, the balance owing said Swaney Frazier, as Captain of the Light-horse-men in Apakshanubbi District, in the year 1844.

Approved October 9, 1845.

A RESOLUTION providing for the pay of certain Claimants.

SEC. 12. *Resolved* by the joint Committee on Claims, That the following persons be paid for hauling iron in Apakshanubbi District, for the three months' shops, viz: Adam Leflore, the sum of fifteen dollars; Noel Gardner, twenty dollars; James Garland thirty-five dollars; and Silas McKinney fifteen dollars.

Approved October 9, 1845.

AN ACT providing for the pay of Willis J. Harkins and George Pusley.

SEC. 13. *Be it enacted, &c.*, That the following persons be paid, viz; Willis Harkins for hire of black-smith tools to the Apakshanubbi District for three months, and hauling the same, twenty-five dollars; also Capt. George Pusley, for the hire of black-smith tools, for the year 1844 and 1845, forty dollars; also Nita-nakni for hire of black-smith tools, for the year 1845, twenty dollars.

Approved October 9, 1845.

AN ACT providing for the pay of Judy, a Chickasaw woman.

SEC. 14. *Be it enacted, &c.*, That Judy, a Chickasaw

woman, be paid three dollars for the use of her house by the National Court, in the year 1845.

Approved October 9, 1845.

AN ACT providing for the pay of Mr. Cochran.

SEC. 15. *Be it enacted, &c.*, That the sum of sixteen dollars be set apart and appropriated to be paid to R. L. Cochran, for the rent of a cabin for the Senate to do business in.

Approved October 9, 1845.

AN ACT appointing Allen Carney to revise the Laws of the Choctaw Nation.

SEC. 16. *Be it enacted, &c.*, That Allen Carney be, and is hereby appointed to revise all the laws of this Nation within four months from the passage of this Act; and to prepare the same for the Press; but he is not to alter or change the spirit or meaning of any portion or part of the original of any of the laws. And that after such revised laws shall be compared and approved of by the General Council, he shall receive for said services one hundred dollars.

Be it further enacted, That the Clerks of the several Districts shall be required to furnish Allen Carney with a full copy of all the laws in their possession without delay.

Approved October 10, 1845.

AN ACT providing for the pay of Creek Delegates.

SEC. 17. *Be it enacted, &c.*, That Nathaniel Folsom, Peter Folsom and Telokey shall each receive ten dollars for their services in going to and returning from the Creek Council, in the Spring of 1845.

Approved October 10, 1845.

[The foregoing acts with the exception of Section third were signed by Thomas Leflore, Nitakache and Isaac Albertson, Chiefs.]

A RESOLUTION authorizing Col. David Folsom to build a Senate House.

Sec. 18. *Resolved*, That Col. David Folsom be requested and authorized to contract for the building of a Senate and National Court House, at Nanihwaiya, of the following dimensions, namely: One room, 18 feet square in the clear, to be built on each side of the Council House, and in a line with the front of the same; to be built of hewed logs and covered with three feet boards well nailed on, good wooden chimneys, lined up to the mantle, with rock backs and jambs; the cracks to be lined with shaved boards; the floors to be laid with jointed but undressed plank; two windows and one door to each room, with plain shutters; and one plain table, three and a half feet square; and two benches to each room. The whole cost of the same not to exceed three or four hundred dollars, which will be paid for by contribution of this Nation. And the said building all to be completed by the meeting of the next General Council.

Approved October 10, 1845.

—

AN ACT providing for the pay of Sintinowa.

Sec. 19. *Be it enacted, &c.*, That the sum of twenty dollars shall be paid to Sintinowa for the use of his blacksmith tools at Boktuklo in Pushimataha District for three months.

Approved October 10, 1845.

—

AN ACT placing the petition of the Orphans in Mushilitubbi District in the hands of the Orphan Agent.

Sec. 20. The Committee, to whom was referred the talk and petition of the Orphans in Mushilitubbi District, have deemed it advisable to place them in the hands of the Orphan Agent, Col. P. P. Pitchlynn.

Approved October, 1845.

AN ACT for electing Treasurers, Auditors, and Supreme Judges in the several Districts of this Nation.

SEC. 21. *Be it enacted, &c.*, That Basil L. Leflore is elected Treasurer, and Lewis Garland Auditor, for Apakshanubbi District.

And be it enacted, That Kennedy McCurtain is elected Treasurer and Adam Nail Auditor for Mushulitubbi District.

And be it further enacted, That William H. Harrison is elected Treasurer and Jerry Wade Auditor for Pushimataha District; and that William Barnet is elected Supreme Judge, Joe Mitchell Treasurer, and James D. Gaines Auditor for Chickasaw District.

Approved October, 1845.

[The foregoing resolution and acts were signed by Thomas Leflore and Isaac Albertson, Chiefs.]

ORPHANS.

Your Commitee, to whom was referred the Petition of the Choctaw orphans, would respectfully recommend that Col. P. P. Pitchlynn be appointed by the Council as Agent in behalf of the petitioners, and to be the bearer of a Memorial from the General Council to the President of the United States, together with a communication from Major William Armstrong also to the President; and to proceed without delay to Washington City, and there to effect a compromise with the original purchasers, or with their authorized Agent, on such terms as may be deemed just and equitable. But it is distinctly understood that said Agent shall not consent to any compromise for a less sum to be paid the orphans than the original purchase money without interest, either on the amount paid into the Treasury of the United States, or on their Bonds, excepting in the case of some few instances, where the purchasers agreed to pay exorbitant prices and are unable to pay; in such cases the aforesaid Agent is authorized to make a compromise for to receive a sum not less than eight or ten dollars per acre. It is also suggested to your honourable body, that when the said Agent shall have effected a compromise, so that the orphans can realize a speedy benefit therefrom, he shall be entitled to receive ten per cent out of the amount paid into the Treasury. It is distinctly understood that Col. Pitchlynn will defray his own expenses, and should he fail to effect a compromise with the purchasers of Mississippi he shall not receive any compensation or hold any claim against the orphans or the Nation.

Approved October 8, 1845.

GENERAL COUNCIL,
October 8th, 1845.

Col. P. P. Pitchlynn,

Sir:—By resolution of the General Council, you are hereby authorized and directed to proceed without delay to Washington City, with such papers as are placed in your hands to lay before the President of the United States, and with his consent and advice you are are fully empowered to effect a compromise with the original purchasers of the Choctaw Orphan lands, provided for under the Treaty of Dancing Rabbit Creek, on such terms as will secure to the said orphans the greatest amount of money; but you are not authorized to receive a less sum than the original purchase money without interest, either on the amount already paid into the Treasury; or on the Bonds of the purchasers; except in the case of a few instances, where the purchasers have agreed to pay exorbitant prices and are unable to comply with their obligation; in such cases you are at liberty to agree upon a sum to be paid, not less than eight or ten dollars per acre.

Approved October 8, 1845.

GENERAL COUNCIL,
October 8, 1845.

To his Excellency, the President of the United States:

The Choctaw General Council respectfully represent that they received petitions from certain of their people who claim lands under the Treaty of Dancing Rabbit Creek as Choctaw orphans; complaining that although fifteen years have elapsed since that treaty was concluded, they have never derived any benefit from the tracts reserved for their use; and praying the Council to urge the Government to adopt measures for their relief.

The Petitioners state that they have been informed, and believe, that land sufficient to satisfy their claims has been set apart and sold for their benefit, on terms requiring the payment of a small portion of the consideration and leaving a large balance unpaid with interest accruing. They further state that the purchasers, when called upon for such balances, have refused payment; alledging that the sales were illegal, inasmuch as they were made under the immediate direction of the President and not by the individual orphan proprietors as the Treaty would seem to intend.

The Petitioners further state they are informed that the purchasers, anxious to avoid litigation, are willing to pay all that is due of the consideration originally stipulated, on condition that the interest which has accrued be remitted; *Provided*, that by so doing they can perfect their titles. Therefore the Petitioners propose that a suitable Agent be authorized to arrange the terms of a compromise, the conditions to be that the purchasers pay over the balances still due, exclusive of interest, to the War Department; to be held in trust until the Choctaw orphans, or their representatives, shall execute a proper instrument, waiving all their real or supposed rights or demands growing out of the alledged illegalities of the former sale, after which to be paid to the proper claimants. This proposition the General Council earnestly request the President to sanction. Since they were first sold the lands in question have materially depreciated in value, and would not again bring the same price.

Whether the objection to those sales on the score of illegalities are well founded or not, a compromise would at least prevent litigation and the consequent delay so prejudicial to the interests of the claimants. It is true that the parties whom the Treaty designed to benefit are no longer in the situation which the term orphan is usually understood to represent. Those who survive have struggled through their minority without the aid they expected to derive from their lands; but most of them are heads of families, and nearly all in destitute circumstances, exposed to the machinations of speculators, who seek to obtain, for little or nothing, their claims both on the Orphan fund at Washington and on the lands in Mississippi; and who, in endeavoring to effect their selfish purposes, not only embarrass those claims and retard their final settlement, but also sow the seeds of discord among our people. And as in duty bound we your petitioners will ever pray.

October 8, 1845.

[The foregoing communications were signed by Joel H. Nail, President of the Senate, Forbis Leflore, Speaker of the House of Representatives; and Thomas Leflore, Nitakache and Isaac Albertson, Chiefs.]

SESSION XIII.—1846.

Sec. 1. *Resolved, &c.*, That the Chiefs are hereby authorized to write a letter to Capt. Armstrong, U. S. Agent, requesting him to refund to Armstrong Academy two hundred and fifty dollars out of the funds appropriated for the pay of Mill Wright.

Approved October 15, 1846.

Sec. 2. *Resolved, &c.*, That our Chiefs be instructed to write to Major William Armstrong to write to the Department, and get them to turn over three thousand dollars and seventeen cents, towards the payment of the debt against Spencer Academy, from the interest funds arising from the funds set apart for the education of forty youths.

Approved October 15, 1846.

Sec. 3. *Resolved, &c.*, That a Committee composed of G. W. Harkins, John Lake and Allen Carney be, and are hereby authorized to receive such portion of thirteen hundred dollars for 1845 and 1846, for the support of the Sabbath Schools, and also to examine the claims and accounts of those Sabbath Schools and pay them, according to the labours they have performed; and the balance, if any remains, shall remain in the hands of the Committee until otherwise appropriated.

Approved October 15, 1846.

Sec. 4. *Resolved, &c.*, That the Chiefs be requested to address a communication to the Agent, requesting him to write on to Washington City, and state to the President that it is the wish of the Council and the Chiefs, that whatever amount of money be standing to the credit of the Orphans may be sent out and paid to said Orphans by the U. S. Agent early as possible.

Approved October 15, 1846.

Sec. 5. *Resolved, &c.*, That the following amounts are hereby allowed to the following persons, viz; to Col. S. D. Fisher, fifteen dollars; to Willis J. Harkins, Capt. George Pusley and Col. Thomas Leflore, twenty dollars each; and fifteen dollars to C. Spring for the hire of Smith tools. And also to Noel Gardner, twenty dollars; Col. Leflore, for fifteen dollars; to Adam Leflore, thirteen and a half dollars; Edmund McKinney, thirty-five dollars, all for hauling iron and steel to the different three months' shops in Apakshanubbi District; also to L. Battiece, nine dollars; to Nowahambi twelve dollars; and to John Adam, nine dollars, all for hauling iron for the Public Shops in Pushimataha District.

Approved October 16, 1846.

Sec. 6. *Resolved, &c.*, That a Committee composed of G. W. Harkins, R. M. Jones, Benjamin Love and Adam Nail, be selected to draw up an Article of Agreement between Mr. F. X. Coincion for the privilege asked for.

Approved October 16, 1846.

Sec. 7. *Resolved, &c.*, That whereas there seems to be some misunderstanding as to where the true Chickasaw District Line commences on Red River, and in consequence of this various difficulties and inconveniences have existed both to the people of Chickasaw District, as well as to Pushimataha District, and must exist until this important question is settled either by the Treaty making powers or by the Government of the United States. The difficulties that have chiefly existed are in relation to the jurisdiction of the Courts, and as to how far the authority of each Chief extends; also there is another difficulty in electing Members to the Council in this disputed space of country, and estimating the population of each District necessary to elect Members to Council according to their ratio, Therefore,

Be it resolved, That the Judicial jurisdiction of the Chickasaw District shall remain at Island Bayou until the District line is definitely settled between Pushimataha and Chickasaw Districts.

Proposed by Benjamin Love.
Approved October 16, 1846.

—

SEC. 8. *Resolved, &c.*, That there be taken out of the $7,000 set apart for National purposes the following sums, viz: to pay the expenses of the Districts, viz:

Pushimataha District,	$1,566 10	
Apakshanubbi District,	1,883 60	
Mushilitubbi District,	446 80—	$3896 50
Senate and Court Houses,	345 00	
To V. Brashears,	9 00	
To Allen Carney, for Revising Laws,	100 00——	454 00
		$4,350 50

Approved October 17, 1846

—

SEC. 9. *Resolved, &c.*, That the thanks of both Houses be tendered to the Superintendents of all the Public Schools in this Nation, and Major William Armstrong, U. S. Agent, for the many services they have rendered to our Nation.

And be it further resolved, That the Clerks of the several Districts be instructed to send a copy of the same to the persons as prescribed in the above resolution within their respective Districts.

By A. Carney.

Approved October 17, 1846.

SEC. 10. *Be it resolved, &c.,* That the Chiefs are hereby requested by the Council to ask the Agent for the Intercourse Laws of the United States relating to Indian Tribes.

Approved October 17, 1846.

SEC. 11. *Resolved, &c.,* That fifty dollars set apart for the payment of P. P. Pitchlynn, as Trustee in Apakshanubbi District, be paid over to G. W. Harkins, as he acted by himself; and as he had all the duties to do we think it right and just that he should receive the fifty dollars.

Proposed by Henry Folsom.

Approved October 17, 1846.

SEC. 12. *Resolved, &c.,* That the $600 allowed to the Choctaws by the United States for timber and rock taken from the Nation for the erection of Fort Smith, be paid over to the four Chiefs, and an equal division made agreeable to the population of each District, to be used for District purposes.

And be it further resolved, That the Chiefs be requested to inform Major Armstrong of the passage of this Act, and request him to reserve it from the Annuity.

Approved October 17, 1846.

SEC. 13. *Resolved, &c.,* That both Houses meet to-day and go into an election for National Judge, Supreme Judges and School Trustees.

By G. W. Harkins.

Approved October 17, 1846.

Noel Gardner is elected National Judge, Kennedy McCurtain is elected Supreme Judge of Mushulitubbi District, and Henry Love for Chickasaw District. And R. M. Jones, G. W. Harkins, Forbis Leflore and Thompson McKinney are elected Trustees.

[The foregoing resolutions were signed by Thomas Leflore, S. D. Fisher, Peter Folsom and James McLaughlin, Chiefs.

INDEX.

SESSION IV.—1837.

SESSION V.—1838.

SESSION VIII.—1841.

SESSION IX.—1842.

SESSION XI.—1844.

SESSION XIII.—1846.

APPENDIX.

SESSION IV.—1837.

SESSION V.—1838.

SESSION VII.—1840.

SESSION VIII.—1841.

SESSION IX.—1842.

SESSION X.—1843.

SESSION XI.—1844.

SESSION XII.—1845.

SESSION XIII.—1846.